SEQUENCE OF ACTION

Court Position

> The server chooses the appropriate court position and prepares to serve.

Going into Motion

> Three distinct actions are started at the same time.

Body	Racket Arm
Weight shifts to back foot.	Arm starts down.
Left knee begins to bend forward.	Arm reaches full down position and starts moving toward backstop.
Body weight remains on back foot.	Arm and racket continue to come around toward cocked position.
Body coil is just beginning.	Arm and elbow almost ready to be cocked.
Body coil is really building. Right knee bends in same direction as left knee.	Elbow bends, arm cocks, wrist cocks, and racket drops behind back.
Body coil is completed including some backbend. Both knees are fully bent.	Arm and racket are in the fully cocked position.
Body weight whips upward and forward as knees begin to straighten. The only contact with the ground is the balls of both feet.	Wrist starts racket upward and forward, right shoulder starts upward and forward. Racket is picking up speed rapidly.
All body weight is being thrust upward and forward at the hit point. Left toe is barely touching the court, as right foot begins to come forward. Body is extended in straight line.	Entire right arm and shoulder are fully extended, wrist has complete triggered and racket head is traveling at its highest speed.

(HIT)

PATTERN PLAY TENNIS

R. SPENCER BRENT

PATTERN PLAY
TENNIS

ILLUSTRATIONS BY
GEORGE JANES

1974

DOUBLEDAY & COMPANY, INC.
GARDEN CITY, NEW YORK

ISBN: 0-385-05874-8
Library of Congress Catalog Card Number 72–89295
Copyright © 1974 by R. Spencer Brent
All Rights Reserved
Printed in the United States of America
First Edition

To Tony Trabert, a long time friend,
who places the importance of helping
young people believe in themselves far
above the goal of teaching them tennis.

CONTENTS

THE AUTHOR

While playing tennis tournaments in Europe and the United States, Spencer Brent got to know most of the tournament players and became close friends with many world champions.

Knowing he someday wanted to teach tennis, he began studying players' strengths and weaknesses and how these related to their basic stroke production. He took notes on what players thought about their own strokes and their opponents'. He paid special attention to ideas and key words that conveyed the mechanics of a stroke with impact and meaning.

He took lessons on how to teach tennis from Les Stoefen, one of the all-time great professional teachers, and then spent several years gaining teaching experience. He worked with Maureen Connolly and the Junior Wightman Cup team the year the roster included such familiar names as Billie Jean (Moffitt) King and Karen (Hantze) Susman. Over the years he experimented and improved on all he had learned about teaching tennis, and from this was born the concept of Pattern Play Tennis.

He first used Pattern Play Tennis in teaching Tory Fretz, who later achieved a national ranking as fourth in the United States. Then he coached Linda Tuero, who won the National

Clay Court Singles Championship and has been ranked seventh in the United States. One of the author's most recent students, after one year of intensive Pattern Play Tennis, entered the Los Angeles City Championship and, although unheard of and un-seeded, reached the finals and upset a nationally ranked player in straight sets to win the tournament.

The author has played national championship tournaments in Europe and the United States, including Forest Hills, and has reached the semi-finals of the nationals in platform tennis.

Mr. Brent is forty-three years old, lives in Scarsdale, N.Y., with his wife, Elaine, and their daughter, Monica, and son, Spencer

PATTERN PLAY TENNIS

INTRODUCTION

Pattern Play Tennis has produced championship players in re-markably short time periods because it is based on a simple but powerful fact . . . *Every point is a pattern.* Trace the flight of the ball during a point and the resulting lines will form a pattern on the court surface. Do this for several points and it becomes obvious patterns repeat themselves.

By using the concept of Pattern Play Teaching combined with a thorough understanding of not only the "how to" but the "why" of each stroke, you can experience the tremendous sense of achievement of seeing a student progress into an outstanding tennis player. And the satisfaction of knowing you have helped someone, I mean really helped, continues every time you see him hit a winning shot, or come home with a trophy, or make the headlines when he upsets a ranked player, or when you team up together and win the club doubles championship.

There is a very definite side benefit to Pattern Play Teaching. You can substantially improve your own game, because by thoroughly understanding the refinements of each stroke and by talking about them over and over again, you will be sur-prised by suddenly playing better yourself. For example, most players are taught to get to the ball with the wrong foot and this robs a great deal of a player's natural power. The fact is the foot that gets the player into position should not be the foot that is part of the hit. By teaching the correct footwork, by having to repeat it over and over again, and by observing the tremendous difference it makes, you will be automatically programing or brainwashing yourself into using better footwork. And there are many other benefit areas besides footwork, so when you want to bring your own game to a new peak, get someone familiar with Pattern Play Teaching to hit patterns to you.

There are many tennis players who are convinced teaching will create bad habits in their own game and therefore refuse to coach anyone, even occasionally. Unless they use Pattern Play Teaching, their concern is well justified. The reason their game suffers is simple. Watching the ball through the hit is very important, and accomplishing this on every shot takes a great deal of self-discipline until it becomes second nature. Teaching breaks this down by requiring the instructor to divide his attention between the student and the ball. He must analyze the student's stroke, and at the same time move into position to hit the ball back to the student. Soon the teacher is "peeking" as he hits, thus opening the floodgates for many bad habits. Yet all of these habits are caused by not watching the ball.

Pattern Play Teaching completely eliminates the tendency to "peek" as the instructor never attempts to return the ball hit by the student.

This book will help you teach the wonderful game of tennis well. It will answer the undeniable prerequisite of having to know the subject thoroughly. It will help you to communicate this knowledge, it will help you to analyze a student's understanding or lack of it, and it will help you to innovate when a learning problem develops. The book is not written with the idea of making thousands upon thousands of tennis players into professional teachers, but it will enable you to bring a student along as far as you wish and up to the point a good teaching professional gets into the act. And this professional will be greatly helped by what has been done before him.

Learning to play tennis takes time and the process is a rather orderly progression of accomplishments. Each stroke chapter follows this progression step by step from basics through stroke refinements, so as your student improves you will be able to move deeper into each chapter introducing new challenges as he becomes a better and better player. As you use Pattern Play Tennis be sure to teach all the strokes to your student each lesson so that his game develops as a well-knit unit.

Apologies are in order to all who are left-handed, for they will have to mirror the instructions, which can get complicated. But, hopefully, having done this through their lives, the task will be a familiar one.

1. *Serve to backhand.*
2. *Backhand return to backhand volley.*
3. *Backhand volley to backhand.*

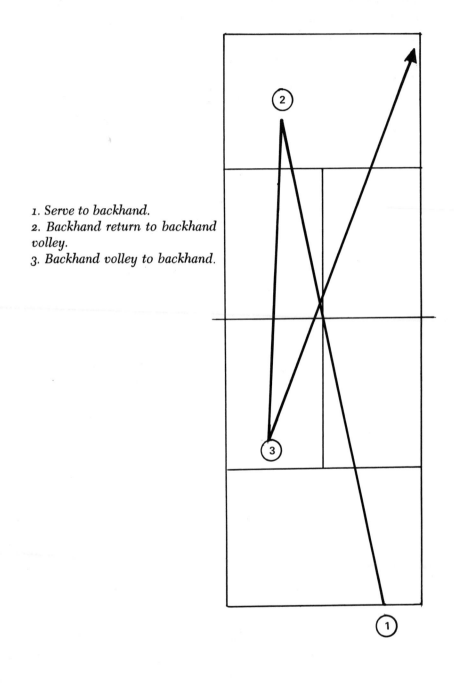

CHAPTER ONE

PATTERN PLAY TEACHING

Patterns in Tennis

To fully appreciate the significance of Pattern Play Teaching, all you would need to do is trace the flight of the ball during a point. If this were done for several games, it would become obvious patterns repeat themselves as you would soon be drawing patterns on top of patterns. For example, how many times have you seen this pattern (*opposite*) repeat itself in a match, set, or even a game?

Using this pattern as a simplified example, it becomes obvious points are made up of patterns, some complicated and some never really getting started, as in the case of a double fault. We could even substitute the word "pattern" for "point" and introduce a new meaning to the game, as in "Who won that last pattern?" Therefore, if any player masters the various patterns that occur during a match, by practicing, learning, and conquering them *one at a time,* he will become an outstanding player. And that is exactly why the concept of Pattern Play Teaching has been so successful.

Pattern Play Teaching's greatest advantage over any other method of teaching is its flexibility. Patterns can be varied in speed, direction, and order of difficulty of shots, or the instructor can duplicate a pattern again and again. This makes it possible to apply Pattern Play Teaching to beginners, intermediates, advanced, and championship players.

Let's take a beginner—one who is just starting off working

on basic stroke production. With the old method of teaching, the ball would be bounced to the forehand over and over again until the student began to get a certain grooved quality to that stroke. And then the backhand would be worked on, over and over again, until that stroke began to feel natural. The unfortunate part of this method of teaching, is there then comes a period during which the two strokes have to be tied together. Grips need changing between shots. Footwork and body movement linking the shots must be learned. And to make matters worse, almost inevitably the backhand falls behind the progress of the forehand. During this phase of joining the shots together the student feels his progress has stopped and will often become discouraged.

Now let's apply Pattern Play Teaching to the same example. The student is asked to face the net at the base line, just as he would if he were about to play a game. The instructor holds four balls in his left hand and hits them to his student one after the other, alternating forehand and backhand, forehand and backhand. He does not attempt to hit any of his student's returns. The instructor begins to mold stroke production within the framework of the way the strokes will be used during play. After stroking the first ball of the pattern, which a new student probably will miss completely, the next ball is on its way, coming to the student's backhand. There simply is not time to worry about a missed shot and the student's concentration does not slacken, nor does he become discouraged.

With a little prompting, and slow patterns, the student is reminded to change grips between shots. Within just a few minutes, you have established a basic rhythm—racket back, forehand swing, change grip, racket back, backhand swing, change grip, racket back, forehand swing, etc. It is that simple, and takes longer to explain it than for the beginner to pick it up. Footwork also becomes a part of Pattern Play Teaching quite naturally. The student will instinctively move into the ball properly when hitting an alternating pattern, for he knows the next shot in the pattern will be to the opposite side. This gets his weight moving through the shot and toward the net as he comes back to the ready position. The patterns are deliberately kept simple and a great deal of time is permitted between shots. The important factor is the student is learning the game as a unit, all together, without interruption, and with a smooth-flowing transition developing from one shot to the next.

Now let's take an example of how a pattern can be used with a top player. Remember, top players, even world champions, are confronted with some of the same problems facing the beginner. Even among the best, strokes will falter from time to time. Footwork, watching the ball, timing, all these need to be constantly worked on to remain in top form. The great Lil'Mo (Maureen Connolly), used to use patterns to sharpen up her game, particularly when she was having a stroke or a footwork problem. One day in particular, she was very unhappy with the way she was moving on the court. She asked that I step up the speed of the patterns to the point that the second ball in the pattern was being sent on its way *before* the ball she had just hit had crossed the net. This picked up the tempo of play to an almost impossible speed. The result was a very considerable improvement in her covering of court under normal play conditions. The idea in this case is not unlike the batter who will pick up a heavily weighted bat and swing it prior to going to the plate.

In summary, we can say that for every problem that plagues a tennis player, whether a beginner or a world champion, an explicit pattern can be picked to work on that problem. And it can be repeated again and again until that problem is mastered.

How to Hit Patterns

In order to hit precise patterns to a student, the best technique is for you to stand about five feet behind the net, holding the racket in one hand and four balls in the other. Your

student is back on his base line at the ready position. Without
bouncing the ball, you then hit the first ball of the pattern to a
predetermined spot. The student moves in and hits that ball,
say, down the side line. As the ball he has just hit reaches the

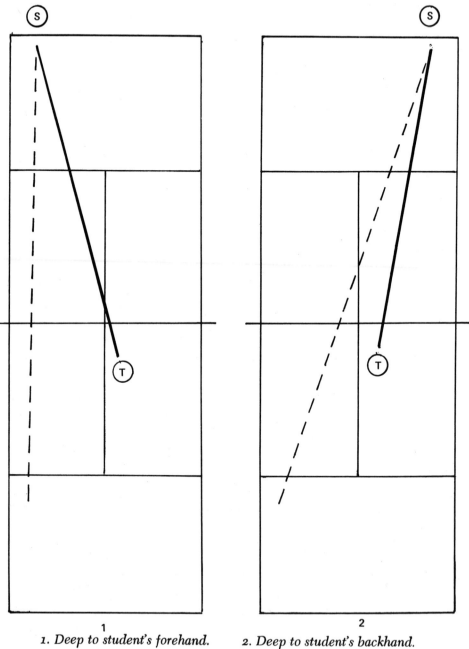

1. *Deep to student's forehand.*   2. *Deep to student's backhand.*

net, and again without bouncing it, you hit the second ball in your hand to the next predetermined point in the court. You do not attempt to return the balls hit by the student. For example:

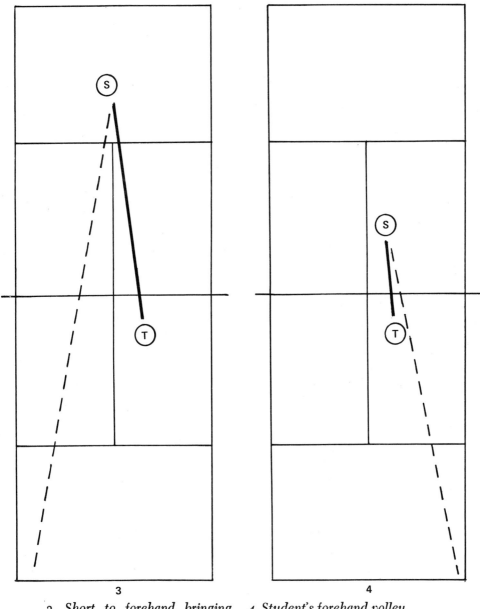

3

4

3. *Short to forehand bringing him to net.*

4. *Student's forehand volley.*

Remember, the objective of Pattern Play Teaching is not to make it so difficult that the student is continually scrambling. For the beginner, you not only stick to a simple pattern, but you also let your student know ahead of time where each ball in the pattern will be hit. If he can get set, at least in his mind, and know in which general direction he will be expected to move, his progress will be much faster.

Selecting Patterns

Initially, patterns can be used to probe various aspects of a student's game. Simple patterns can progress into more difficult ones, until finally, errors begin to occur. At this point, a specific problem can be selected and the degree of difficulty of the pattern can be adjusted to then work on that problem. The amount of time you wait before you hit the second ball, how hard you hit it, where you hit it, and finally where you have asked your student to return it, all can be varied depending on the degree of ability of your student. Now let's take an example.

Let's suppose you have an intermediate student who is consistently missing an approach shot off his forehand during a series of patterns. The chances are if your student were asked to hit one isolated approach shot from that position in the court, he wouldn't miss too often. But now, you mix this shot into a realistic pattern that includes an approach shot. In the preceding diagrams the "trouble" shot would be in *Diagram* 3. In going to work on the problem you could use the same pattern. The first pattern shot is a forehand, followed by a backhand, and finally, the shot he's been missing. But as he hits it he knows it will be followed by a volley, and so the pressure is on, just as it is during play.

To further develop this example, let's say you hit several identical patterns, checking all the basics, one by one. After isolating what you think the reason is for his missing the approach shot, you hit several more patterns, just to make sure. At this point you are certain the basics are being performed properly with the exception of his watching the ball. So you point this fact out, tell him to keep his head down and watch the ball through the hit, and then go back and redo the pattern with him concentrating on watching the ball. If you have correctly diagnosed the problem, his progress will be quite startling. Stick with this pattern until it has been mastered. The feeling of accomplishment is another benefit of Pattern Play Teaching.

Without exception the best way to teach a student is to hit patterns on every basic stroke every lesson. While progress may seem slow, actually it will be just the opposite, for your student will be learning the game as a well-knit unit. From every stroke that must be learned by a beginner to every problem that can plague a top player, a pattern can be created to work on that stroke or problem. Further, the degree of difficulty of a specific pattern may be varied from very easy, to difficult, to impossible, just by increasing the speed of the shots and/or decreasing the time interval between each shot. As you teach, using patterns, you will find it increasingly easy to create new ones to solve a problem or help teach a stroke. Be flexible and use your imagination.

CHAPTER TWO

THE VOLLEY

The best place to introduce your student to Pattern Play Teaching is at net, as the volley is a relatively simple stroke. His progress will be quite noticeable even on the first lesson, and this will give him confidence in you and his ability to learn the game. In each subsequent lesson you will always cover all the strokes so that his game progresses as a unit.

Grip

Even if your student is not a beginner, check his volley grip carefully. Most players, not realizing it, use the wrong grip and greatly handicap their net play as a result. The correct volley grip is the Eastern backhand, also called the Continental, and it is used by virtually all of the top players. It has many advantages, not the least of which is both backhand and forehand volleys are made with the exact same grip, which is particularly valuable during a fast exchange of shots.

Starting a student out on the Continental grip will undoubtedly cause learning problems on the forehand side. But be stubborn, hang in there, and together you will win out, for conquering the Continental is mostly mind over matter and establishing racket face control with the wrist. The benefits to your student of going this route are well worth the extra effort many times over. If you come across a student who after quite a few lessons is just not making any progress, then the reluctant alternative is to move his grip toward the Eastern forehand, and then gradually over a period of time bring him back to the Continental.

As the Eastern forehand grip is the easiest to get exactly right, introduce it to him first. Ask him to take the throat of the racket in his left hand and place the palm of his right hand flat against the strings. Have him slide his right hand, with fingers outstretched, down the racket making sure the palm remains parallel with the strings. When his hand reaches the handle he simply closes his fingers around it (*Figure 1*). The butt end of the racket should extend slightly beyond the heel of the hand.

Now he is ready to learn the Eastern backhand, which is also called the Continental. Ask him to look down at his Eastern forehand grip and note the position of the "V" formed by his thumb and forefinger in relation to the racket head and handle (*Figure 2*). To attain the Continental grip he moves the "V" ¼ turn to his left. The palm of the hand moves from parallel to the racket strings to a position almost completely on top of the handle. As a result the "V" is now to the left of the handle (*Figure 3*).

While this is the correct grip for all volleys including the overhead, there is a minor modification that can help your student learn the Continental on the forehand volley. The modification is simply this, the heel of the hand does not come quite as far on top of the handle, although the rest of the grip remains the same. This grip can be used on both backhand and forehand volleys.

Before leaving the various grips, the modified Continental should be covered. It is simply a grip position that is halfway between the Eastern forehand grip and the full Continental or Eastern backhand grip. The grip is a compromise and can be used on all volleys as well as on the backhand ground stroke. It should not be used on the forehand. For a player that just cannot master the full Continental grip on the volley, the modified Continental is an acceptable compromise.

Figure 1. The Eastern forehand grip is like shaking hands with the racket. The fingers should be spread a little for better racket control.

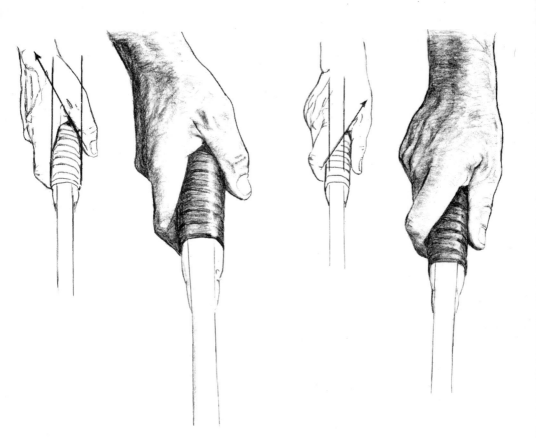

Figure 2. (Left) Although there are modifications of the Eastern forehand grip, the only stroke it is used on is the forehand.

Figure 3. (Right) With the exception of the forehand, the Continental grip is used on all strokes including volleys, half-volleys, overheads, serves, and backhands. Depending on the stroke and the player's preference, the thumb can be wrapped around the handle, or as shown here, placed almost parallel to it.

Figure 4. In the ready position the right elbow should be tucked in close to the body and the right hand should be forward and inside of the right hip.

Ready Position

Because of the extreme shortness of preparation time at net, the ready position takes on added importance. Be critical of your student if he does not get this part of the volley learned and learned well.

Move him to a position of 8 to 9 feet behind the net straddling the center service line. His weight should be evenly distributed on the balls of both feet which should be spread about shoulder's width apart. His knees ought to be flexed, and even though his body is slightly bent at the waist, his rump should be tucked in under him. His right hand should be belt high, holding the racket with the correct volley grip. The left hand cradles the throat of the racket so that the racket head is forward and in front of the left shoulder area. The face of the racket must be perpendicular to the court surface. He must have his concentration under complete control and be ready to spring into instant action, but his muscles should not be rigid (*Figure 4*). While all this sounds easy, it will take plenty of practice before he is doing it well.

Basic Stroke

The volley, either backhand or forehand, is an abbreviated and relatively simple stroke, although body weight and footwork are very important. Show your student how simple the racket movement actually is.

FOREHAND

From the ready position have your student move the racket head to his right, laying his wrist back sharply, bringing the racket parallel to the net. His elbow should be bent and kept tucked in fairly close to his body. His forearm should be

Figure 5. Laying the wrist back sharply and making it solid as a piece of steel is the answer to learning the forehand volley using the Continental grip.

forward of and to the right of his hip. Even though he is using the Continental grip he should have no trouble in positioning the racket face in an open position of approximately 35 to 40 degrees. The head of the racket should be slightly above the handle (*Figure 5*).

BACKHAND

Have him bring his racket back to the ready position, and after checking the grip to make sure it is still correct, have

Figure 6. Great strength is built into the backhand volley by positioning the forearm well forward and by keeping the wrist absolutely solid through the entire shot.

your student move the racket to the backhand volley position. The basic difference between this and the forehand volley is the wrist is not laid back when moving the racket parallel to the net. Instead, racket position is accomplished through a rotation of the wrist and forearm so that the back of the hand is facing skyward. The racket hand is in front of the body instead of off to one side. As with the forehand volley, the racket face is open (*Figure 6*).

Figure 7. When footwork is introduced, the left hip moves forward but the shoulders remain parallel to the net.

FOOTWORK

Before hitting volley patterns to your student, you need to demonstrate the footwork. Ask him to take the ready position. Then, moving the racket to the forehand volley position as practiced earlier, have him take a short step forward and to the right with his left foot. If a line were drawn from the toe of his right foot to the toe of his left foot, it would be almost perpendicular to the net (*Figure 7*).

Figure 8. On the backhand volley, shoulder pivot is pronounced as the left shoulder moves to the rear and the right shoulder moves forward. The hit point must be well toward the net.

Now have your student come back to the ready position. Have him move the racket to the backhand volley position while stepping forward and to the left with his right foot. The movement of the shoulders is quite pronounced. A line drawn from the toe of the left foot to the toe of the right foot will be almost perpendicular to the net (*Figure 8*).

Bring your student back to the ready position. At this point have him put it all together, moving quickly from the ready position to the forehand volley, back to the ready position, to the backhand volley and back to the ready position. Repeat this without pausing and he will quickly establish a rhythm that is like a simple dance step.

EASY PATTERNS

By now your student is probably wondering if he is ever going to hit a ball, but the preceding steps will prove well worth the time and effort.

Move back to your service line and hit soft alternating patterns with the first shot going to the forehand, the second to the backhand and so on. All your student does on each shot is repeat the racket movement and footwork you have just shown him, moving the racket directly in front of the path of the ball and keeping his wrist absolutely firm. Make sure you give him time to come back to the ready position after each ball, but keep the rhythm of your shots consistent so he will begin to pick up a sense of timing.

While the net is a good place to start a student, the difficulty of your hitting patterns is greater, for the target area you hit each ball to is fairly small (*Figure 4-R*). In addition, your shots will strike the net more often as it will be directly in front of your student. If this happens too often the rhythm of your patterns will be disrupted and the best solution is to move closer to net, but hit your shots with less pace. If you are working with a beginner, you may want to do this anyway, or even toss patterns to him. As he progresses you can begin hitting them, and as he improves you can move a few feet farther away from net hitting patterns from a still deeper court position. By moving in stages like this over a period of several lessons, you will find a beginner adjusts quite easily.

The first problem you will run into is the tendency of your student to swing at the ball. The minute you see him doing this, remind him his racket is, in the beginning, simply to be a

Figure 4-R. Due to the difference in shoulder pivot, the backhand target area is closer to the student than the forehand.

firm backstop that he moves in front of the oncoming ball. As your initial patterns should be soft, the momentum of the ball will not always be enough to carry it back over the net after hitting your student's racket, so be sure he is convinced you are not concerned with his getting the ball back over the net. Emphasize that for the first few lessons you are primarily interested in his establishing racket position, body weight, and footwork. If you do not make this clear, he will be concentrating on getting the ball back any way he can, and this defeats one of the big advantages of Pattern Play Teaching.

Hitting in Front

The importance of hitting the volley in front of the body cannot be overstated, and there are several reasons why. First, getting body weight in behind a volley comes naturally when the ball is hit early, but is virtually impossible if the racket is allowed to get jammed up against the stomach on the hit. Second, judging the speed and trajectory of the ball is far easier when the racket contacts the ball in front of the body. Third, the arm and racket are easier to move and have much greater strength when extended forward. Fourth, the player has a wide choice as to where he can volley his return if the hit point is well in front of him.

To thoroughly impress your student with this, take a piece of chalk if you are on a hard court, or a stick if on clay, and draw a line parallel to the net just in front of your student's feet. Draw a second parallel line to this one so the lines are apart about 6 inches less than the length of a racket. With his toes on the first line, ask your student to get in the ready position. The head of the racket should be directly over the second line (*Figure 9*). Point this out and explain you want him to reach forward and volley the ball *before* it gets to the first line, even though he will be starting from behind the second (*Figure 10*).

Figures 9 and 10. The parallel lines give a reference point and a good idea of what is meant by hitting the ball early and in front of a player's ready position.

The Punch

Now comes the fun part of the volley. For a change, start with the backhand volley instead of the forehand. This way the student does not begin to get a complex about either stroke. From the ready position have him move the racket to the backhand volley position. Without letting the racket move back of the line just in front of his toes, have him pull the handle of the racket down and forward, keeping the wrist very firm. He should stop this motion just as sharply as it was started with a total of about 8 to 12 inches of travel. Too big a follow-through leads to inaccuracy and an inability to be ready for the next shot during a fast exchange, so be sure to correct him every time he moves the racket more than 12 inches. The only time a big follow-through is used is on a high put-away volley where speed needs to be imparted to the ball.

Have your student move back to the ready position before trying the forehand volley. The punch and power in the forehand volley comes from the shoulder and forearm. The motion is similar to a very short stroke on a handsaw or a boxing jab. The basic movement is between the hand and elbow with limited shoulder movement. The wrist is locked and rigid and does not change from its laid back position.

You are now ready to tie the punch and footwork together. This time as he moves the racket into the backhand volley position, have him take the short step you have practiced before, and in addition as his weight moves forward, activate the short forward and downward punch. Have him return to the ready position and do the same thing on the forehand side. Repeat this walk-through exercise until he is doing it smoothly.

Now you are ready to hit alternating patterns, with your student practicing the short punch on both the backhand and the forehand volleys without any pause in between. Be ready to stop and make corrections if he starts to swing. Be sure he understands the racket should not be brought back behind the line in front of his toes and in fact should be kept well in front of it and simply moved forward into the flight path of the ball.

Body weight is the key to a powerful volley and the next procedure is very effective in giving your student an idea of just what you mean. Have him face the net in his ready position. Stand facing him far enough away so when you extend your arm the palm of your hand is about 6 inches from his right shoulder. Ask him to lean his weight against your hand without moving his feet. Be ready to support some of his weight so he doesn't lose his balance. The feeling he has of almost falling forward while leaning against your hand is the same feeling he should have as he begins to move forward to intercept a ball on the volley. This is true even if there is not enough time to execute proper footwork.

Now, quickly move your hand away and he will have to take a quick short step forward to catch himself. His stepping forward with considerable body momentum is the same feeling he will have just as he hits the ball. Now he knows how it should feel.

Putting all of this together will take time and plenty of practice, but once he is consistently volleying easy patterns, you should without telling him, gradually increase the speed of your shots. What will happen is your student will begin to make some good, firm crisp volleys that really zing across the net, and both of you will feel the excitement of knowing a major step has been accomplished.

Random Patterns

Up to this point your patterns have been directed at establishing the basic volley. Now it is time to make things a little tougher pattern-wise.

You have been hitting alternating shots and your student has known in advance where the next shot was coming. In hitting random patterns, you mix up your shots, thus taking this advantage away from him.

You can start a pattern off on either backhand or forehand, and then hit two consecutive shots to the same side. This is going to mess up his net playing rather dramatically, so it is best to warn him. One approach that works well is to say, "Okay, you're hitting good solid volleys, but I'll bet I can make you miss by not hitting to alternate sides. I'll even hit the shots a little softer, but you won't know which side they will be coming to. Is it a bet?" If your student is eager, he will tell you how he will hit every shot as well as before. But knowing where the next shot is going before it is hit is a very big advantage.

Pattern Play Teaching should be fun. Take the time to make a game of random patterns. Mix them up while he tries to out-guess you. Will he figure where the last shot is going if you have already hit three in a row to his backhand? If you fool him, kid him a little and he will respond to the challenge.

This accomplishes two things. First, he will begin to learn anticipation. Instinctively, he will start to watch you as you hit each shot, searching for little indicators or giveaways as to where you are going to hit the ball. Secondly, the challenge will stimulate his interest for he will recognize this step as a big one toward actual play.

Be patient if he starts missing badly, for his attention is being divided for the first time. If he continues to have trouble, go back to a few alternating patterns to re-establish his confidence.

Lateral Movement

This series of patterns is so critical, if a player does not master it his net play will be severely limited. The pattern series has two objectives. The first is footwork. Specifically, not what foot to start off on, but how to arrive at the hit point on the correct foot. The second objective is to get him to crowd the ball so he is getting full body weight in behind each volley.

FOOTWORK

The basic footwork being introduced at this point carries into all other strokes and sets the stage for an offensive player, or if not properly learned, a defensive player. The concept is simple and extremely important. The foot that gets the player into position should not be the foot that is part of the hit. If he learns this early, he will be mentally programed not to rely on the hitting foot to get him to the ball.

To reach the objective of this pattern series you must make your student move parallel with the net in order to get to the ball. All you have to do is hit each shot one step farther to his left or right than you have been doing. Keep them waist high as before and hit your shots softly so he has plenty of time. As this lateral movement will be quite strange to him, go back to alternating patterns so he will know in advance where your shots will be coming.

The key to your student's mastering this new dimension is for him to understand what he is expected to do. He must move quickly for a wide shot and achieve a new position that then becomes the same, relative to the flight of the ball, as all the pattern shots he has been handling. That sounds easy except all previous footwork during the volley involved just one foot crossing over and forward. Now he must first take an additional step.

Before hitting any wide patterns it is a good idea to walk through the footwork. Taking the backhand for example, get your student in the ready position. Ask him to take a step to his left with his left foot and plant it firmly. Bring the right foot toward the left foot, but instead of planting it, he starts the hit part of the volley. His weight shifts toward the net, moving off the left foot as he comes forward to contact the ball

Figure 11. The foot that gets the player into position should not be the foot that is part of the hit, but in this case the right foot is doing double duty. As a result, body weight is going toward the side line instead of into the hit.

exactly as he has done in all the previous patterns. Bring him back to the ready position and have him walk through the forehand volley starting off with the right foot. Practice this by moving first to the backhand then to the forehand without pausing at the ready position. Repeat this until he is moving smoothly.

You should now go back to your normal court position from which you have been hitting patterns and ask your student to walk through the footwork one more time. As he does this, make a mental note about how far his initial step carries him. Aim your pattern shots just wide of that point. After the completion of each pattern your student should be closer to the net than when he started. This means he is moving into the ball properly and that he'll have to move back before starting another pattern.

This pattern series should be practiced over and over again until he is consistently moving into the volley with the correct foot. As your student starts getting very good, you need to push him hard by increasing pattern difficulty. Lateral movement is the enemy of a well-executed volley and each player strives to make his opponent stretch wide for a shot and then follow-up the resulting advantage (*Figure 11*). Your patterns should do exactly the same thing so he gets to be an expert on achieving a new strong position prior to his volley. When he has mastered this it will be tough for an opponent to force him at net.

CROWDING THE BALL

The final refinement in volleying and the difference between a very good volleyer and a great one, is learning to crowd the ball. Not only does this make it easy to put plenty of pace on the ball, but it also makes it difficult for an opponent to anticipate what direction the volley will be hit.

In the first two examples, over-all position is very good (*Figure 12, Figure 13*). The racket is well forward toward the net and both footwork and body balance are excellent. But in both examples the ball is being played off to one side and full body weight will not be available on either shot. In addition, but equally important, is the fact that in both situations the ball can be easily volleyed down the side line, but the degree of difficulty in going cross-court is increased by quite a bit. Because of this, and particularly if the oncoming ball has been really well hit, the volleyer will play the percentage shot down the side line. The problem is an experienced opponent will see this and in most cases correctly anticipate the direction of the volley.

Figure 12. The racket is well forward toward the net and both foot-work and body balance are excellent. But in both examples the ball is being played off to one side and full body weight will not be available on either shot.

Figure 13.

Figure 14.

In the second two examples, everything is the same in terms of footwork and body balance, but the ball has been crowded (*Figure 14*, *Figure 15*). As a result, full body weight will be behind each shot regardless of what direction it is hit. And be-

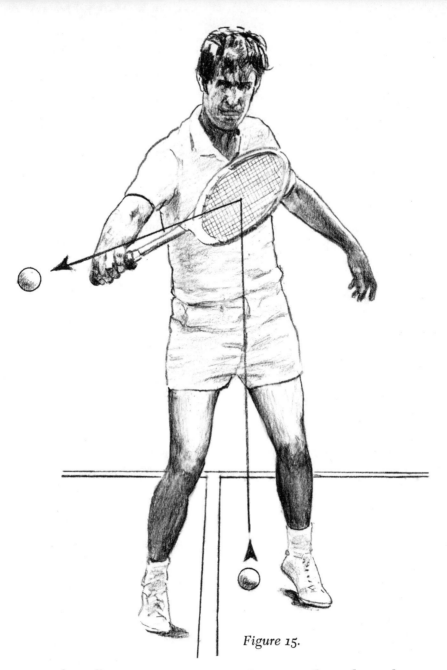

Figure 15.

cause the volleyer can go cross-court just as easily as down the line, his opponent's anticipation will be reduced to pure guess-work.

In this series of patterns ask your student to hit all of his returns cross-court. This will really put the pressure on him to start fast and intercept the ball well in front of him. If he does not crowd the ball he will not be able to consistently cross-court his volleys.

Once his footwork and body balance become well established you can move to random patterns. When his quickness in getting to the ball shows obvious improvement, you should increase the speed of your shots making it even tougher. Challenge your student, push him, keep him digging hard, but above all make sure he is crowding the ball and his weight is moving into the shot. If he starts faltering on the tougher patterns, ease off until he gets going and then press him again.

Low And High Volleys

As your student begins to master the volley, he will instinctively learn to open the racket face more on low volleys and on those made from deeper than normal court positions. But watch closely to make sure he does not drop his racket head below the level of his racket hand. This is a bad habit that is very easy to get into particularly on low shots. Instead, he should bend his knees, occasionally to the point the trailing knee almost touches the court.

At the same time you should get him in the habit of getting his eyes down to the level of the oncoming ball by bending his knees. This results in the big advantage of being able to better judge speed and direction of the ball, and as a bonus gets him down for a low shot well before the hit. The last step is to make sure he stays down on the volley through the entire shot. If he straightens up during the hit, the effect is similar to carefully sighting a rifle and then standing up just as the trigger is pulled.

On high volleys he will soon learn to close the racket face and hit down on the ball. He will also learn the higher the volley, the more vertical the shaft of the racket will become in order to reach the ball. As he gets good at hitting volleys at shoulder level or higher, you can get him to use some wrist movement to impart additional speed.

Approach Shot—First Volley

During actual play, the first volley is the toughest and most critical, and if it is weak the odds swing heavily against the net rusher. But the key to a successful first volley is the approach shot. Whether it is a serve, serve return, or a ground stroke off of an opponent's shallow ball, the approach shot must be deep and well placed. The net rusher should come in behind it on a line that bisects the angle of the several possible shots his opponent can safely make. As he comes to net on that line, he should skip or land on the balls of both feet, much like in hopscotch, in the general area of the service line. There he should hesitate for a split second and judge exactly where his opponent's return is going and then move in to make his first volley. Although this brief pause is performed by all top players it is not apparent unless you are looking for it, but during a tournament on grass, a worn area soon appears just in front of the service line as proof positive.

When you are ready to work on your student's approach shot, a very effective pattern series is to start with the first two shots as ground strokes followed by two volleys. For example, get your student to assume the ready position behind the base line. Hit your first shot fairly deep to his forehand as you would on a normal ground stroke pattern series. Your second shot will be 8 to 10 feet short of the base line, say to his backhand. This is the approach shot, and he should move in on it hit it deep, and come to net. The third ball of the pattern he should handle as a volley just inside the service line area, and the fourth and last ball should also be a volley.

CHAPTER THREE

THE SERVE

The serve is without question the most important stroke in a player's weaponry. It can win a point outright, or at least set the stage so the odds of winning it are overwhelmingly in favor of the server. If the server can accomplish this on a high percentage of points, he will consistently win his serve. If he wins it each time he serves, he cannot possibly lose.

Like they say, nothing worthwhile comes easily, and that goes double for the serve, for it is by far the most complicated and difficult shot to master. What makes it complicated is the server is required to perform separate and seemingly disassociated actions which result in transmitting maximum racket energy to the ball. In addition, spin is introduced for the first time as a major and critical component of a stroke, and to put heavy spin on a ball the racket must travel dramatically away from the direction the ball is to go.

Before getting into what spin actually does to the flight of the ball, it will help to understand the relationship of spin, speed, and placement. No matter how well placed a serve may be, if it has no speed and is just a blooper, any good player will move in and kill it. Add enough speed to a well-placed serve, and the result is an ace. That sounds easy enough except the high-speed flat serve has no spin, and spin is control. That is why the flat serve is impossible to hit with a high degree of accuracy. Put another way, if a top tournament player were allowed only one serve, he would seldom risk the flat high-speed serve, knowing if he missed with it the point would be over. Without spin he cannot control the ball. With spin he not only can consistently place it where he wants it, but he can aim it much higher over the net and have it still come in, and even though the ball is traveling forward with less speed, the spin keeps it from being a setup.

The frustrating part is, the server cannot have maximum speed and maximum spin at the same time. He can build up just so much racket speed or energy, and that's it. He can channel all of it to speed and no spin, resulting in the flat cannon-ball serve. Or he can convert most of it to spin and very little forward speed, as in the case of the American twist. He can select any mix between these two extremes he wants, but as he increases speed, spin must decrease, and with it control. See *Diagrams A* and *B*.

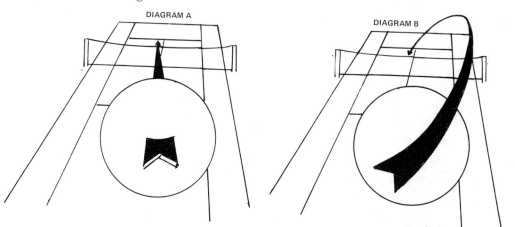

Diagram A. Flat serve has little margin of error. Diagram B. Spin serve has large margin of error.

In this age of rapid technological break-throughs, understanding how and why something happens, rather than accepting it at face value, is one of the key principles that makes break-throughs possible. When applied to the serve, this principle has resulted in some surprising break-throughs, not only with students but with seasoned players who have been plagued with serving problems. It centers on the fact that many players do not understand how spin controls the flight of the ball. They are instructed to hit up skyward more if the ball is going too long. They are told to get their racket moving more to the right because this will make the ball curve left. The problem is these instructions seem to contradict what has been learned on the ground strokes where they were taught to follow through in the direction they want the ball to go. So it takes time to mentally accept this. What happens is they listen to what they are supposed to do, but they have difficulty in doing it. A perfect example is getting a student who is serving well with the forehand grip, to shift to the Continental. The problem is not physical, for he is perfectly capable of swinging the racket properly. The real problem is the Continental grip and resulting racket face angle just do not make sense to him, and so when he uses the new grip he runs into trouble. The fact is, the moment he really accepts how spin works and why the Continental grip is necessary, his progress will be rapid.

Spin controls and steers the ball very accurately. It does so because the velocity on the ball is the sum of the forward speed plus or minus the spinning speed. Forward motion and spin combine to create two different air pressure areas. One side of the ball experiences a wind velocity equal to its translational velocity *plus* spinning velocity. The other side experiences translational velocity *minus* the spinning velocity. A technical point of interest is a ball spinning at any speed, fast or slow, will not curve if it does not also have forward motion.

Looking at the front side of the ball as you would be doing if returning serve, air pressure builds up on the front half that is spinning toward you and decreases on the front half spinning away from you. In *Diagram C* the air pressure builds up on the left side of the ball and decreases on the right side, causing the ball to curve from your left to your right, as in the case of a slice serve. Depending on how the racket hits the ball, this axis can be tilted in varying amounts. In the case of the spin serve in *Diagram D*, the axis of rotation has been

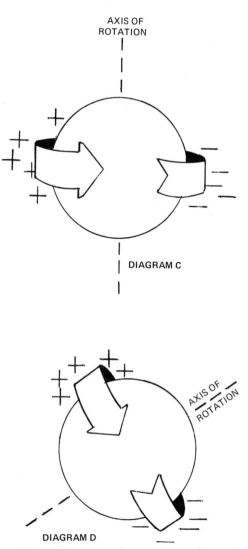

AXIS OF
ROTATION

DIAGRAM C

AXIS OF
ROTATION

DIAGRAM D

tilted and the ball will curve down, as well as from left to right.

Where your student will benefit the most from this is he will understand how spin controls the ball, that the control is precise and unchanging being based on a mathematical formula, and that to impart spin to a ball the racket must travel in a different direction from the desired flight path of the ball. As a result he will have a clear picture of not only what he must do to develop a good serve, but why.

SEQUENCE OF ACTION

Court Position

The server chooses the appropriate court position and prepares to serve.

Going into Motion

Three distinct actions are started at the same time.

Tossing Arm	Body	Racket Arm
1. Arm starts down.	Weight shifts to back foot.	Arm starts down.
2. Arm descends to just below waist-high position and then starts back up, shoulder starts up.	Left knee begins to bend forward.	Arm reaches full down position and starts moving toward back-stop.
3. Arm is almost at full height although elbow is still slightly bent.	Body weight remains on back foot.	Arm and racket continue to come around toward cocked position.
4. Arm is fully extended and ball leaves fingertips. Left shoulder has moved to its highest position.	Body coil is just beginning.	Arm and elbow almost ready to be cocked.
5. Left arm remains fully extended in "Statue of Liberty" fashion.	Body coil is really building. Right knee bends in same direction as left knee.	Elbow bends, arm cocks, wrist cocks, and racket drops behind back.
6. Left arm remains extended for balance.	Body coil is completed including some backbend. Both knees are fully bent.	Arm and racket are in the fully cocked position.
7. Left arm begins to move down out of the way.	Body weight whips upward and forward as knees begin to straighten. The only contact with the ground is the balls of both feet.	Wrist starts racket upward and forward, right shoulder starts upward and forward. Racket is picking up speed rapidly.
8. Left arm has moved completely out of the way.	All body weight is being thrust upward and forward at the hit point. Left toe is barely touching the court, as right foot begins to come forward. Body is extended in straight line.	Entire right arm and shoulder are fully extended, wrist has completely triggered and racket head is traveling at its highest speed.

HIT

Serve Sequence of Action

Every ounce of a server's concentration and muscular ability should be directed toward transferring maximum racket energy and accuracy into the service delivery. To accomplish this he must perform several independent actions simultaneously. Each of these actions will be covered in detail and should be taught to your student separately, one at a time, until he can put them together and still perform each action well. Even if your student is not a beginner, substantial serve advancement can be made by improving each action independently.

It will help if you show your student the sequence-of-action chart, as it will allow him to visualize the interrelationship and timing and how each action you teach him fits together with the others.

Court Position

Ask your student to step up to the base line 1 or 2 feet to the right of center line. His left foot should be at a 45-degree angle to the base line and 2 inches behind it. The right foot is parallel to the base line but about 12 inches to 18 inches behind it, or in other words, his feet are about shoulder's width apart. The right foot's position relative to the left one is one-half step closer to the right side line.

As you work on his serve, it is a good idea to switch service courts from time to time. When you move him over to the backhand service court, your student's position is slightly different. Get him accustomed to this right in the beginning. To serve to the backhand court, the server's position is 3 feet to 4 feet left of center line and the right foot should be moved back about one-half step farther from the right side line although still parallel with the base line. This turns the body a few more degrees to compensate for the different angle between the server and the backhand service court.

Stance

Each time your student prepares to serve, the first thing you should check for is his being tense. Make sure his hand holding the tennis ball is not rigid and that the racket hand has not tightened to a white knuckle grip. Really emphasize the importance of being relaxed during preparation for the serve. This is one of the critical factors in developing a consistently big serve for any player, for the ability of muscles to spring into fast smooth action greatly depends on the counterpart muscles being completely relaxed. One set of muscles does not have to "let go" before the others take over.

Tenseness, by getting one muscle pulling against another, not only causes service faults and robs power, but during a match is very tiring and can take the edge off a player's entire game. The trouble is, tenseness can become a habit, and the worst part is a player can become increasingly tense during a match without realizing it. If you teach your student to check for his being tense each time he prepares to serve, he will learn to control it. As he learns to control it on the serve, he will be able to do the same on other strokes. Thus his entire game benefits, particularly on the two most important strokes, the serve and serve return. In time this check for tenseness and subsequent relaxing of the muscles will become a habit, and he will only occasionally have to remind himself to relax. Being relaxed has begun to become part of his game.

As your student takes the ready position prior to serving, his body weight can be on the back foot or evenly distributed on both. The arms are not extended forward away from his body, but hang comfortably by it. The right forearm is approximately parallel to the court surface and therefore the right hand is waist high. The right elbow is tucked in close to the body (*Figure 16*). The left hand, besides holding the tennis balls, cradles the throat of the racket on the tips of the last two fingers. The ball that is about to be tossed, is resting on the tips of the first two fingers and thumb. If a second ball is being held it is well into the palm of the hand (*Figure 17*).

The racket is pointing in the direction of the service court with the face perpendicular to the ground, and the head of the racket is slightly higher than the handle. If the feet are properly positioned the body is sideways to the net. The entire stance should be comfortable and relaxed.

Figure 16. (Left) Being completely relaxed and at the same time having mental concentration at its peak takes plenty of practice.

Figure 17. (Right) The toss can make or break a serve and how the ball is held can make or break the toss.

Grip

The Continental or Eastern backhand grip is the one used by top players, but many students have trouble learning with it. Although there are problems with starting your student on the correct serving grip, there are some advantages too. The answer is a compromise.

Start him with the backhand grip even though he will probably run into trouble. After he has struggled for ten or fifteen minutes, give in and move the grip a little bit toward the forehand. Stick with this new grip for the rest of the serving part of the lesson. You probably will have to compromise and give ground toward the forehand once or twice more on subsequent lessons, but be stingy about it. Somewhere down the line he will begin to get the hang of it with a grip that is not too far away from the correct backhand grip. This is a lot better procedure than automatically going all the way to the incorrect forehand grip when starting a student out on learning to serve.

Toss/Tossing Arm

Most service problems result from inaccurate tosses. Take any of the best servers in the game and mess up the toss and you'll see poor serves and plenty of double faults (*Figure 18*).

To toss a ball with the left hand is tough enough, but to complicate matters, the server has the racket arm moving, body weight will soon be shifting, and finally the area the ball is being tossed to is quite small. There is only one solution to the challenge—lots of practice.

Explain to your student the importance of extreme accuracy in the toss. The ball should be hit 12 inches forward of the base line and 6 inches to his right. Take some chalk or a stick if it's a clay court and outline his left foot. Next get him to toss

Figure 18. The toss should lay the ball up "dead." This is accomplished by using all arm and no wrist or finger flick. The tossing arm should end up in the "Statue of Liberty" position.

the ball as if he were serving. Let him go through all the motions of the serve but do not let him hit the ball with the racket. Allow the ball to drop and mark the spot where it hits the court. A handful of pennies works well. Your student then places his left foot in exactly the same place as marked by the outline, and repeats the procedure. Do this about twelve times. Now draw a circle to include all the pennies or marks, which probably will be all over, including behind him. The circle is usually 5 feet in diameter (*Diagram E*).

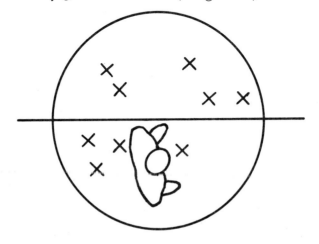

You can demonstrate your point further by asking him to move up into his hitting position with his arm and racket fully extended to the correct hit point. Then indicate where the ball would have been at its peak and the direction it would have been going to land on one of the marked spots behind him. He will quickly see how impossible it would have been to have hit the ball correctly on that particular toss.

Whether you play a great deal of tennis or not, get by yourself and try tossing the ball, marking where it hits the court. It will give you full appreciation of just how difficult the toss can be even without the stroke complicating it further.

Get your student to practice the toss. As an "assignment" you can give him the challenge of seeing if by the next lesson he can get at least half of his tosses into a 12-inch diameter circle you will draw for him, the center of which will be 12 inches forward of the base line and 6 inches to the right of his ready position (*Diagram F*). As you work with your student on his toss, there are several points you should be watching for.

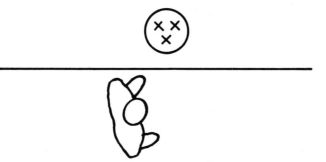

1. The ball to be tossed is held on the tips of the first two fingers and thumb.
2. It is held so gently the fuzz on the ball is not even bent.
3. The tossing hand is completely relaxed.
4. On the toss, the left hand moves forward and up in the direction the body is facing, rather than toward the net or parallel with the base line.
5. The arm motion is like trying to toss an egg up on a pillow so that it lands softly and stays there.
6. The toss is sufficiently high so the racket and arm can come from the cocked position and hit the ball at a point high enough so both arm and racket are fully extended.

Hitting Position

Even with an advanced player considerable improvement can be made on the serve by practicing this next step. Get your student into the relaxed ready position and give him a very old beat up racket. Have him use his normal serve grip and place the racket head down behind him much as if he were scratching an itch in the small of his back. Get him to relax. You should be able to take the racket right out of his hand! His shoulders are turned and his right elbow should be pointing toward the fence in back of him (*Figure 19*). From this point have him throw the racket up and out triggering his wrist so the racket travels end over end. If the keeper of the courts screams at this point, you can accomplish the same thing by tossing the racket in an open field. This exercise is particularly effective with girls, as most boys have been throwing things for years. The important action to watch for is the wrist starting the racket head on its way up and out (*Figure 20*). Your student will soon have a very good idea of how it feels to properly trigger the racket and that the throwing action is very close to the actual serve.

The First "Hit"

Now you are ready to tie the toss and the hit together. One of the best ways is with another old racket that has had the strings removed. What this does is eliminate a very big psychological hang-up on the part of the student as to "where the ball is going to go." Although this may border on being a gimmick, the important thing is it works, and works well. It is just as effective with a more advanced student who is having serving problems as it is with the beginner.

The student assumes the ready position with the stringless racket in the cocked position. Check again for being relaxed. Have him toss the ball and "hit" it. If done properly the ball will pass right through the middle of the racket head. As the student comes through with his wrist and body, the ball should hit him in the area of his right shoulder blade. Repeat this again and again until the toss is accurate and the wrist is triggering nicely. The arm and body should be extended in a straight line at the hit point. The student should get the feeling he is pulling his shirt tail out stretching for the ball.

Figure 19. (Left) By far the best way to develop a top serve is to start off learning it in the back-scratch position.

Figure 20. (Right) When the wrist triggers, it throws the racket upward and forward at the ball.

When your student has the serve actions pretty well co-ordinated starting from the back-scratch position, the next step is to hand him his own racket. Don't make any comment that he will be hitting with a strung racket, just switch rackets and have him serve. The odds are he will hit some good serves right from the start. If he loses the timing, go back briefly to the stringless racket until he gets the feel of it again. You probably will have to perform this racket switch several times, but the procedure is very effective.

Racket Arm/Full Wind-up

Although there is no rush, you will want to get your student using a full wind-up. Before you do this, he should be well grooved and hitting serves consistantly from the back-scratch position. His toss should be accurate, he should have a fair amount of power, and most important, he should be able to place the ball into the forehand and backhand areas of both service courts. How long it will take before he gets to this point depends on his athletic ability and how hard he has practiced on his serve. If he has worked hard, you may find he is ready within three to four weeks. If he has not practiced and played that much, it can take several months.

When he is ready, the best way to accomplish the step to a full swing is to again use the stringless racket. At first, get him to practice the full backswing, tossing arm as well, but without a ball. Devote special attention to bringing the racket from the ready position down past the waist, out parallel and pointing toward the back-stop, and around and up into the fully cocked back-scratch position. Have him repeat this until it becomes a smooth continuous motion. Do not allow racket face to close on backswing (*Figures 21, 22*).

Now you are ready to put it together with the ball, actual toss and stringless racket "hit." In the beginning he will have some difficulty in getting the timing of the racket and the ball to coincide at the correct hit point. But the stringless racket will help get him past this obstacle quickly. When you are satisfied that he is performing all the actions of the serve properly, it is time to hand him his own racket and actually hit some serves. Watch carefully for the following:

1. The racket arm starts down simultaneously with the tossing arm. The motion of the arm and racket is like a pendulum and is continuous. The racket face should be opened slightly during backswing.
2. The arm, wrist, and hand remain relaxed. The wrist remains uncocked.
3. The arm and racket extend out to a position pointing toward the backstop and are parallel, at that instant, to the playing surface At this point the tossing arm should be almost fully extended and the ball is starting to leave the fingertips.
4. The elbow bends, the wrist cocks, and the racket head drops to the back-scratch position. The arm, wrist, and hand remain relatively relaxed.

Each time he properly executes these four steps, he will find himself in the familiar back-scratch position. If he has previously grooved his serve from this position, he will find the transition very easy. There should be no pause in his swing when going from the ready position, through the backswing to the back-scratch position and into the hit. With very little practice your student will be hitting good serves with a much better sense of timing and with considerably more power.

Body/Coil

In the beginning your student will have plenty to think about between the tossing arm and the racket arm. But once you have moved him to a full backswing and he is getting that pretty well grooved, you will want to start refining his body actions. Body/coil adds finesse and power that marks the top

Figure 21. Closing the racket face on the backswing faces the wrist downward, making it awkward for the wrist and arm to cock when the racket drops into the back-scratch position.

Figure 22. The face of the racket should be at least perpendicular to the court and preferably slightly open.

server. It is not difficult for your student to learn if you get him working on it at this point.

The key to developing body/coil is the understanding by your student that he is throwing the racket up skyward toward the hit point as well as forward. To accomplish this with maximum power he must employ some backbend and subsequent pulling or snapping of the body forward with the stomach muscles. As this is occurring, he should also be getting additional thrust from the knees straightening and pushing upward from a bent position to a straight position (*Figure 23*). When these actions are combined with the triggering of the racket and arm toward the hit point, the result is a tremendous amount of power.

Follow-through

When the server unleashes all the striking power he has in his coiled body and cocked arm, then his weight is thrust upward and forward resulting in quite a bit of momentum. This momentum should be allowed to bring the racket arm and body right on through in a big free follow-through. Restricting or holding back the follow-through can rob power and accuracy.

As your student serves watch for the following points on his follow-through:

1. The arm and racket power right through the hit point and continue forward and down finishing across the left leg. This should be a big free motion.
2. The right shoulder follows and ends up moving forward and pointing down at the court in the area of the left foot.
3. The right foot follows across the base line into the court toward the service court being served to.
4. The entire follow-through is big, free, and not too different from the follow-through of a professional baseball pitcher.
   Although the work horse is the spin serve, in top tennis it is

Figure 23. As body/coil builds and just prior to the hit, both knees should bend in the same direction.

important to be able to hit the slice, flat, and American twist serves. However, do not introduce these to your student too soon, for all this will do is confuse him and mess him up on his spin serve. If your student is a beginner, wait until he has had a minimum of two years to develop and groove his basic spin serve. When you do start teaching a student the other serves, always include several minutes of brush-up on his spin serve, thus keeping it grooved and solid.

Slice

The only basic difference between one spin serve and another is the angle of the axis of rotation. As discussed previously, the slice serve's axis of rotation is almost vertical. In order to impart this spin, the racket must strike the ball with comparatively little upward thrust and a great deal of sidespin. So the racket can impact the ball at the proper angle, your student must shift his toss 6 to 8 inches to the right of the spin serve's hit point. In addition to being moved to the right, the toss and the hit point are a few inches lower than on the other serves. The grip, however, does not change.

Starting from the ready position, the racket arm performs the same backswing right on through to the cocked back-scratch position. But from this cocked position, the racket head spoons around the right hand side of the ball striking it at the three o'clock position (*Figure 24*). Put another way, instead of traveling upward and directly forward, the racket moves more toward the server's right and contacts the outside edge of the ball. Its momentum brings it sharply around the far side of the ball and then travels in a more horizontal right to left follow-through finishing up on the server's left side. Different from the other serves, the elbow is somewhat bent at the hit point.

Figure 24. At the hit point on the slice serve, the racket is per-pendicular to the court while the arm is much closer to being hori-zontal.

American Twist

The American twist serve is quite different from the slice as its axis of rotation is tilted sharply to the left. To impart the American twist spin, the racket must contact the ball at the eight o'clock position and travel up and outward toward the two o'clock position. To make this easier to do, the toss is moved to directly over the server's head. Get your student to practice this new toss until he is consistent, then he is ready to start hitting.

Up to the cocked position and except for the toss, all the motions are the same as the other serves with possibly a little more backbend. The grip is the same as on the other serves. At the back-scratch position your student's wrist should trigger the racket up and to the right. His arm straightens upward and to the right just as if he were trying to toss his racket in the top of a tall tree that is forward and to his right just outside the fence. Although the arm should be fully extended at the hit point, because of the ball's position directly over the server's head, the racket shaft will be at about a 45-degree angle to the racket arm. This is quite different from the flat serve where the racket shaft is vertical. This angle allows the wrist to trigger the racket up from the underside position of the ball and it is at this point the racket is traveling at its highest speed. After the hit the racket continues upward and toward the right side-line fence (*Figure 25*). Then in follow-through, it starts downward ending up on the server's right side. This is the only serve the racket does not cross over in front of the server's body during follow-through.

Almost all of the racket's power is directed toward spinning the ball and very little of it goes into forward speed. This does not mean less energy or effort is put into it, for the twist serve should be hit with everything the server has got.

Figure 25. A split second before the wrist triggers, the racket is at a 45-degree angle with the arm. After the wrist triggers and even though the arm is moving, the racket overtakes and passes it with tremendous speed.

Flat

Unlike all the other serves, the flat serve has no spin to bring it into the service court and therefore it must pass very close to the net, which means the margin of error is not very big. Players under 6 feet should not depend on an absolutely flat serve, as the shorter the server the less the margin of error. Depending on the individual's height and ability, he can reduce spin and increase speed up to the point he starts faulting. He should consider this serve his "flat" serve. If he is tall enough and has the ability, he may actually get to the absolutely flat serve.

There are only a few adjustments to be made to hit a flat serve. The toss is a little farther to the right than a spin serve, but not as far as the slice. At the hit the racket shaft is vertical and therefore a straight-line extension of the racket arm. And finally, the wrist is turned outward so the face of the racket hits the ball absolutely flat (*Figure 26*). Everything else from ready position and grip, to backswing and follow-through remains the same as the basic spin serve.

Summary

The answer to developing a consistent and forcing serve is good solid instruction and lots of practice. Considerably more practice than on any other stroke. But just going out and serving a whole bunch of balls won't do it. The kind of practice that will do it is the hard work variety. This means your student must analyze each serve he hits, which in turn means he should question how well he is performing each part of the serve. "How good was that last toss? Am I triggering my wrist? Let's see what happens if I move my hit point up just a little higher." He, in effect, takes over your role as instructor,

Figure 26. Stretching as high as possible for the hit point gains valuable inches that increase the safety margin over the net and frees up power.

and although he can't see himself, he most certainly can feel when he does something right or wrong. Most important he can work on accuracy.

The best way for your student to improve serve accuracy is to hit at a target. He should take four empty tennis ball cans and put one in each corner of the two service courts. They should be placed on their sides and positioned so they are broadside to him when he is serving. Now he has a target to go for, but emphasize he must not peek during the hit to see if the serve is going to blast one of the cans. That is the advantage in using tennis cans versus some other target, for when he hits one he does not have to see it, he will hear it. Somehow there is great satisfaction in blasting one all the way to the backstop, and you will find the tennis-can target not only keeps your student's interest up, but also builds his confidence each time he hits one.

As your student really starts getting good, you will be occasionally faced with a collapse of one of his strokes and an entire lesson will be spent correcting the problem. But the serve is much too important to neglect, so make sure it gets a good workout every lesson, no matter what.

Serve Patterns

There are several patterns that can help your student's serve once he has his swing fairly well grooved. Different from the patterns used on all the other strokes, the serve patterns' only objective is to link his serve to the rest of his game.

Each serve pattern starts off with your student hitting a serve immediately followed by the pattern you have selected. As you will be hitting these from your base line, try to time the first shot just as if you had returned his serve. In the beginning he will serve plenty of faults as he will be thinking too much about his first ground stroke while he is in the process of hitting the serve. Emphasize the importance of concentrating on the serve and that after he has completed his follow-through there is plenty of time to think about his next shot.

You can use any combination of pattern shots, although if he is a beginner do not use any patterns that include a volley as his first shot of the pattern. Once he has developed good consistency and is ready to start coming to net behind his serve, then it is time to introduce patterns involving a volley immediately following his serve.

CHAPTER FOUR

THE OVERHEAD

A well-hit overhead is a picture of grace, blazing speed, and finality. To the beginner the overhead looks fairly easy, but it is one of the tough ones, and with good reason. In the serving chapter great emphasis has been placed on the toss, for it determines where the hit point will be. If the hit point is wrong, the serve will be at best ineffective. The same is true of the overhead. The hit point is critical. The obvious difference on the overhead is the player must move his body into exact position relative to the flight of the ball. If he does not achieve the correct position, his hit point will be wrong and the effect will be the same as a bad toss on the serve. Plenty of practice will win out, for your student will eventually learn to judge angle of trajectory, speed, spin, and even the wind if it is a factor.

Hitting the Overhead

As the overhead stroke is identical to the flat serve from the back-scratch position, you should not start your student on the overhead until he has grooved his service swing reasonably well. This does not mean he has to be putting his serve in every time he hits it. What you are looking for is good consistency in his swing. If you try teaching the overhead before he has achieved this, his progress will be painfully slow.

Up to this point your student's attention has been directed

entirely to the basic spin serve. To make the adjustment to the overhead a little easier, get him to hit a few relatively flat serves. All he has to do is turn his wrist outward so the face of the racket contacts the ball flatter, and move his toss and hit point a few inches to the right so that on impact the arm and racket are in a straight line and fully extended. Don't spend too much time on this as a deep lob should be hit with some spin anyway. Be very sure he keeps the correct Continental serving grip for his overhead.

Ask your student to take up his ready position 6 to 9 feet from the net just as if you were going to hit volley patterns to him. Instead, you will hit very easy lobs that are as much right to him as you can make them. As you hit the lob he should immediately turn his shoulders and drop the racket into the back-scratch position without any wind-up at all. His left arm should be extended and it is a good idea to get him in the habit of actually pointing at the ball (*Figure 27*). This not only gives him better depth perception, but it automatically turns his shoulders to the correct position. His right leg should be bent so he can push off and move his weight forward into the hit (*Figure 28*). From this point on, everything else is exactly like the flat serve except the problem of timing. Because of the speed of the descending ball he will have a tough time connecting, and so the best procedure is to start him off with a very abbreviated punch-type swing. When your student starts his swing from the back-scratch position, his arm straightens and becomes fully extended, but instead of snapping the wrist forward, ask him to block the ball firmly. His follow-through should end well above shoulder level instead of finishing down by the left shin. Stay with this punch-type overhead until he is consistently accomplishing good hitting position, is timing the ball well, and is placing them with considerable accuracy. When he has reached this point, you can get him to snap his wrist and lengthen his follow-through a bit more, but do this in stages so he does not lose it.

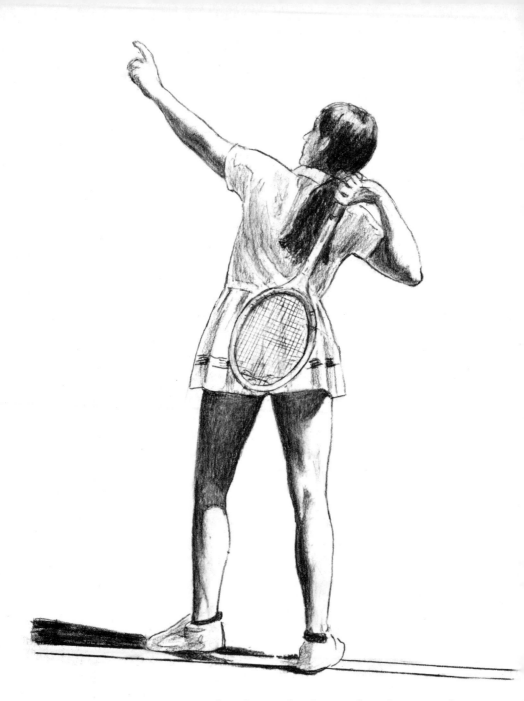

Figure 27. Learning to hit the overhead is made a lot easier by starting in the back-scratch position.

Figure 28. As the ball approaches the hit point, body weight will shift forward and upward as the legs straighten and the wrist triggers the racket. The shoulders remain sideways to the net until the racket and arm bring them around.

Moving Under the Lob

As your student develops his timing, you can begin to make him move a little in order to get into position. As you do this, work hard on the following points:

1. No matter how lazy the lob looks, he should move instantly and fast. The saying "Hurry up and wait" is exactly what he should do on every overhead.

2. When he must move any distance to get under a lob, he should turn and run, looking over his shoulder at the ball just as an outfielder does in baseball. He should watch the ball like a hawk the entire time it is in the air, and especially through the hit.

3. As he digs hard to get under a lob, the head of the racket should be positioned just by his right ear. This places the right arm in a natural running position and also puts the racket close to the fully cocked position (*Figure 29*). When he gets to the point he must turn around to hit the overhead, the racket simply drops from the ear position into the backscratch position.

4. If he has enough time to get into good position he should be back far enough so that his body weight will be going toward the net during the hit. He should stop and wait for the ball in the fully cocked hitting position, but he should not get set for the shot too soon as he must be able to make last split-second adjustments in his position.

5. He should reach up and meet the ball so his arm and racket are fully extended. The hit point should be well in front of him, and his full weight should be moving into the hit.

Figure 29. (Opposite) To get into hitting position under a deep lob, a player must turn and run, but at the same time get his racket and shoulders in position for the hit.

Summary

There are only two situations when a lob should be bounced and then hit. First, and obviously, when it is out of reach. Second, when a player is absolutely certain that by bouncing the lob he can achieve perfect hitting position, still hit it as an overhead, and hit it for a winner. Otherwise the lob should always be hit as an overhead or volley before it bounces (*Figure 30*).

A player's hitting position determines how much power he should put into an overhead. If it is marginal, he should elect to hit the overhead with moderate speed and place it deep into his opponent's court. Although he gives up the chance of a winner, he eliminates the strong possibility of hitting his overhead out or into the net. Depending on his opponent's court position, he may also elect to hit a soft but well-angled overhead. In either case, the key element is placement, not speed.

There is no question speed adds a great deal to the effectiveness of an overhead, but it cannot be successfully included unless the player has good hitting position on the lob and has developed consistent accuracy with his overhead. Don't let your student get into the habit of trying to blast every overhead he hits. This is particularly true on lobs that catch him back of his service line. When this happens he should hit his overhead with some spin, with moderate speed, and return the ball deep into his opponent's court.

There are a few times a lob should be hit as a volley instead of an overhead. As your student's overhead starts getting grooved, you should begin to introduce these volley situations to him.

1. If a player is surprised by a quick lob over his left shoulder and he cannot get into position to hit it as an overhead, then rather than give up his net position, he should take it as a high backhand volley. He should not try to hit this shot hard, but return it deep, or soft and well angled.

Figure 30. When a lob is too deep to reach any other way, a player must leap and time the hit to perfection.

Figure 31. If the hit point is too low, arm and body action becomes cramped and unco-ordinated, resulting in loss of power and accuracy.

2. If a lob is too low to be hit as an overhead, then it should be volleyed (*Figure 31*). The closer this occurs to the net, the better the chances of going for a winner.

Lob Patterns

As you start your student on learning the overhead, you should hit easy lob patterns right to him. They should not be very high and he should have plenty of time between each lob. As with other strokes, once he begins to get the basics nailed down, it is time to increase the degree of difficulty of the patterns. Eventually you will want to duplicate every pattern that occurs in actual play.

To start with you can mix in drives with your lobs. At first you will want to hit these well within easy reach, but as he conquers these patterns you can begin to move him around more. Here is a good basic pattern that is tougher than it looks. Hit the first shot as a drive which he should volley, then hit your next shot as a good lob moving him back from net several steps. After he hits the overhead, hit a weak drive which he should move right back into net and volley, followed by a short lob as the last shot of the pattern series. Use your imagination in creating patterns, and be alert for any particular pattern that gives him trouble. When you find one, go to work on it until it is conquered.

CHAPTER FIVE

GROUND STROKES

All "ground strokes" from serve returns to lobs are based on the forehand and backhand strokes. Therefore, if a player has an erratic forehand, the odds are he will also have an erratic forehand lob or serve return or both.

The importance of solid ground strokes is further emphasized by the fact a player's ground game will only be as formidable as its weakest stroke. Coupled to a weak backhand, a strong forehand can be de-fanged completely by an experienced player.

Preparation

To develop a powerful ground game a player must do three things before he ever hits the ball and he must do them without having to think about it. First he must physically and mentally be ready to move the split second he sees where his opponent's shot is going. Second he must change grips, if necessary, and start his racket back as he pivots. Finally, he must arrive at the hit point on balance and on the proper foot.

If he accomplishes these actions he is well prepared for the hit part of the shot.

Time, or lack of it, is the enemy of preparation. If a player can force his opponent in the early stages of a stroke so his opponent is not prepared for the hit, he is well on his way to winning the point.

On the other hand if a player has learned to save valuable split seconds during his preparation, he will be much tougher to force into errors. Just like a sprinter or swimmer who practices starts, a tennis player should practice preparation until he excels at it.

Before hitting any patterns, emphasize the importance of proper preparation and how it will inevitably affect the outcome of each ground stroke. Make very sure your student understands and accepts this, for his mental attitude toward preparation is just as important as the physical execution of it. He must develop an eagerness, an impatience to get to the ball as fast as possible well prepared for the hit.

Explain the three steps of preparation separately, but combine them when you start hitting patterns for they should be executed in one continuous smooth flow and are easily learned that way.

1. *The Ready Position:* Ask your student to stand a foot behind the base line facing the net. His body should be slightly bent at the waist. His weight should be evenly distributed on the balls of his feet which should be about 18 inches apart. His knees should be flexed and his rump should be tucked well in under him so he can get moving fast.

He should cradle the throat of the racket in his left hand positioning the racket head slightly to the left of the center of his body just below shoulder level. The face of the racket should be perpendicular to the playing surface. His right hand should be belt high close to the mid-point of his body and should grip the racket with either the forehand or backhand grip. (See chapter on the volley for proper grip.) As there is a fraction of a second less time available on the backhand stroke, particularly on serve return, some top players make the backhand grip their standard ready position grip.

While his muscles are ready to spring into instant action he should not be rigid. His concentration should be under complete control and focused on the ball.

Figure 32. After one or two unsuccessful tries to throw a racket over the net, a beginner will take a big wind-up which will result in a natural, compact, and well-executed pivot.

2. *The Pivot:* The pivot is simple except it must be started the split second a player sees where his opponent's shot is coming. He then must change his grip, if necessary, while starting his racket back. The action of the racket coming back helps rotate the shoulders into their proper position. It will be a very big step if you can get your student thinking of his racket as the starter button to the series of actions that make up the pivot.

At the same time the racket starts back and the shoulders rotate, the body weight should start shifting so he can push off hard for the spot he will intercept and hit the ball.

Figure 33. When throwing the racket on the backhand side, a beginner will instinctively execute good footwork and body action even to the point of correctly holding shoulders and hips.

Occasionally you will find a beginner who just can't get the feel of the pivot. This happens most often with girls who have not played other sports much. They have not learned how to wind-up and really let fly with a baseball bat or golf club or whatever. The quickest solution is to grab an old racket that can be thrown and head for an open field. Ask your student to take the ready position, correct grip and all. Get well off to one side just in case. Have him aim for a distant spot, go into a pivot, and heave the racket as he takes a step forward (*Figures 32, 33*). If he has been having trouble with the pivot, the racket will not have gone very far. Kid him and urge him to wind up and really let it fly. Have him try this on both sides, backhand and forehand. As he gets the feel of the pivot he will begin to get his shoulders well around and his footwork and body balance will improve. Now see if you can get him to stop action by yelling "hold it" when he's completed his pivot but before he has started his throw. If you have been fast enough to catch him in this correct wind-up position you can demonstrate all of the points of his pivot he has not been accomplishing on the tennis court. If you feel your student can benefit by additional racket throwing, repeat the procedure. This time get him to take several running steps as if he were intercepting a ball and then heave the

Figure 34. Using the hitting foot to get to the ball means body weight is moving toward the side line. This substantially increases the degree of difficulty in hitting the ball cross-court, a fact an opponent can successfully gamble on.

racket. If during later lessons the pivot begins to deteriorate, head back for the open spaces for a few minutes of racket tossing.

3. *Footwork:* Arriving at the hit point on the correct foot is essential for a strong ground game. The importance of this has been covered in the chapter on the volley, but is so important it is worth reviewing.

The foot that gets the player into position should not be the foot that is part of the hit (*Figures 34, 35*). This allows the final and hitting step to be made in the direction of the opponent's court. To accomplish this consistently a player must be mentally programed not to rely on the hitting foot to get him to the ball.

Figure 35. Getting into position with the correct foot requires just one more step, which can be accomplished by a fraction of a second quicker start and a determination not to get to the ball any other way.

BASIC PATTERNS

Explain to your student the purpose of these patterns is to begin to groove the ready position, pivot and footwork. Getting the ball over the net will come soon enough. Be prepared to repeatedly remind him of this, for in spite of what you say his only thought will be to hit the ball back any way he can. Once he begins to concentrate on his ready position, pivot and footwork, progress will be quite rapid.

If your student is just starting out, it will help to toss the patterns. Move to a position of 10 feet in front of the net on his side of the net and put him one-half step behind his base line. Toss alternating patterns, but give him plenty of time in between the shots so he can get back to the ready position. Keep the time interval or pattern rhythm constant. If he really messes up on a shot, finish the pattern anyway. This will help him learn to recover and keep on going.

In the first series of alternating patterns you will hit or toss each ball so he must take one step to the side, immediately followed by a second step toward the net as he hits the ball (*Figure 36*). Explain to him this is the same procedure he practiced at net. Walk through an example. Show him when you toss the ball to his right he will step with the right foot more or less parallel with the base line and then move forward into the hit with his left foot. You probably will have to adjust your toss point until you find where the ball needs to land for him to best accomplish the correct footwork.

In a relatively short time your student will begin to develop a rhythm. Ready position, change grips, racket back on pivot, forehand swing, to the ready position, change grips, racket back on pivot, backhand swing, and so on. Soon the three basics of preparation will start to blend and become a smoother and more continuous action.

By now your student should be connecting on a few shots. If not, ask him to keep his head down and eyes on the ball through the hit. So he does not get anxious and tighten up, remind him you are still working on preparation.

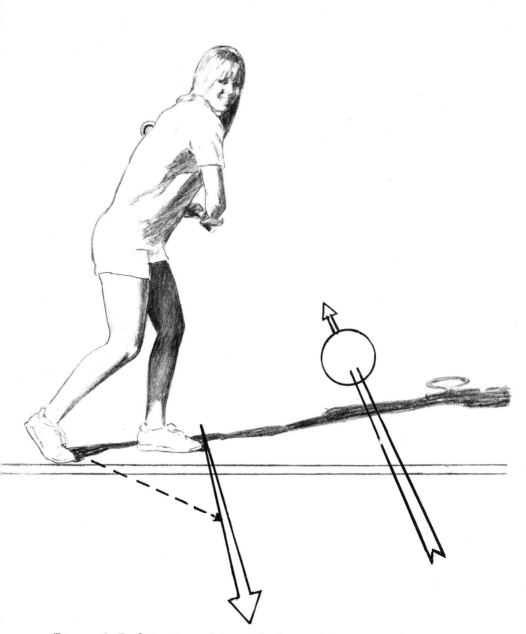

Figure 36. By being in position with the non-hitting foot, the ball can be hit with power and accuracy either cross-court or down the side line. And an opponent does not know which.

Now you are ready to move back on the other side of the net. Two things will happen. First, the ball will bounce differently and he will need to adjust. Second, you will not be as accurate with your patterns which will create some footwork problems. But the solution is easy.

BASIC PATTERNS—FOOTWORK

To a beginner, arriving at the hit point on the proper foot when the ball isn't exactly where it is "supposed" to be is confusing. He will often try to approach the problem mathematically. "Let's see, four steps should take me about there, so do I start off on the left or right foot?" Disaster.

The answer is simple. Continue to hit alternating patterns but hit them farther to each side than you have been. Your student will thus be forced to take more than one step to get to the ball. Make the patterns easy so he will have plenty of time.

He will adjust quickly to this multiple footwork if you can get him to do two things. First, he must be concentrating hard on the fact his hitting step will be toward the net. Second he must get to the ball with very short, almost choppy steps. If he is taking very short, quick steps and if he is thinking about the last step being toward the net, he will automatically adjust his footwork so he gets to the ball on the correct foot. In other words, short rapid steps make adjustment easy. Long strides do just the opposite.

Strokes

BASICS

The backhand and forehand, both being ground strokes, have many similarities from the start of the pivot right through the hit and follow-through. In fact there are very few major differences. Therefore, although the strokes can be taught separately, there are three big advantages to first teaching the similarities of both strokes at the same time.

The first advantage is that learning the common points of the backhand and forehand at the same time continues the joining together of the two strokes into a single unit, with no seams and no mental pictures of the backhand being different and automatically weaker. Second, a single point that applies to both strokes is quickly understood and makes more of an impression on the student than learning the same point separately for each stroke. For example, instructing your student to "watch the ball through the hit" is just as applicable to the forehand as it is to the backhand. As you hit alternating patterns you can get him concentrating exclusively on the problem of watching the ball, thus nailing it down on both strokes. Third, the more clearly your student understands the entire structure of his ground strokes the easier it will be for him to analyze and correct stroke problems that will plague him from time to time. In other words, having a clear picture of the many basic stroke similarities as separate from the few unique refinements of each stroke will help him analyze and correct stroke problems.

Basic Common Points Between Forehand and Backhand

1. From the ready position racket movement should start the instant it is determined which side the ball will be played on. The racket is the starter button for all subsequent actions.
2. The ball is watched from the instant it leaves the opponent's racket right through the hit point.

Figure 37.

Figure 38.

3. If necessary the grip is changed as the left hand guides the racket back. The left hand helps to move and support the racket. In the early stages of the pivot it helps the shoulders turn properly.
4. The speed of the pivot, including the backswing, is determined by the speed of the oncoming ball.
5. As the shoulders continue to pivot smoothly with the arms

Figure 39.

and racket, body weight begins to really get moving in the direction of the point of ball intercept.

6. As the pivot continues, the racket head is brought by the body at about shoulder level on its way to the full back-swing position. The wrist is not allowed to cock upward, which would position the racket shaft much too perpendicular with the ground.

Figure 40.

7. Without pausing the racket starts a descent to hitting level describing a small arc as it does so.

8. Although the swing is continuous, at this instant the racket has reached the full backswing position and is pointing at the backstop. The racket arm is almost fully extended but

Figure 41.

not quite as there is still a slight bend in the elbow. The back foot is planted holding full body weight.

9. The knees should be flexed so the player is well down to the flight level of the ball. He must stay down at that level throughout the entire stroke.

Figure 42.

10. The racket begins to smoothly accelerate forward reaching its maximum speed at the hit point.
11. As the racket starts its forward motion, weight begins to shift to the front foot which has stepped toward the net.
12. The racket shaft is parallel with the playing surface. This is

Figure 43.

particularly important on low shots. The exceptions are shots at shoulder level or higher.

13. At the moment of impact the wrist should be firm. The racket is parallel with the net.

14. At exactly the moment of impact full weight transfer occurs from the back foot to the front foot.

Figure 44.

15. The racket sweeps through the hit in a long follow-through as if the edge of the hand were dusting a long table. As this follow-through occurs, the body continues to move forward thus greatly increasing the length of time the ball is in contact with the racket.

16. During the follow-through the arm becomes fully extended, although it is not rigid nor is the elbow allowed to lock.

Figure 45.

17. The shoulders pivot freely out of the way.
18. The back foot does not swing forward on the hit or follow-through but remains to the rear in light contact with the court thus assuring good balance and a smooth stroke.
19. The racket continues through in its sweep and begins moving upward until it finishes the stroke pointing at the top of the opponent's backstop.
20. At the end of the follow-through the back foot moves forward. This is the first motion toward moving into the ready position in preparation for the opponent's next shot.

All of these twenty basic points apply to both backhand and forehand. As you hit alternating patterns you should cover each point on both strokes right down the list. Not only should your student be able to perform the twenty basics, but he should know them by heart.

During the many lessons needed on basics it is predictable one stroke will come ahead faster than the other. It is very important to catch this early and bring the lagging stroke up. This can easily be done by increasing the emphasis of instruction on that stroke.

Your student has a lot to think about so make sure he is performing these basics fairly consistently before beginning work on stroke refinements.

Stroke Refinements—Backhand

The backhand can be a powerful flowing stroke capable of producing accuracy as well as explosive speed (*Figure 46*). For a very few top players a devastating backhand has become their trade-mark. For some others their backhands are as good or almost as good as their forehands. But for the large majority of players the backhand is a problem and it sets the stage for ultimately losing many, many points. While this is the way it is, it does not have to be. The few reasons the backhand becomes the weakest ground stroke may be dealt with and overcome during the early stages of learning the game.

Points to be discussed with your student prior to hitting patterns on backhand stroke refinements

In teaching backhand stroke refinements to your student, the first step is to overcome the backhand mental barrier. The following points will help him understand why most players'

Figure 46. There is tremendous natural power in the backhand if, and only if, the preparation of the stroke has been properly executed.

backhands are the weakest ground stroke and why his does not have to be. In fact show him why it can be better than the forehand. If he is convinced, together you can forge a backhand opponents will fear, not pounce upon.

1. During the period any beginner was first getting interested in tennis, he undoubtedly watched others play and listened when they talked. It is no surprise he quickly learned the backhand is the weak stroke. His subconscious conclusion is "My backhand will be a problem too." And his approach to learning the stroke automatically becomes a very negative one which often is not obvious, but it's there. Your first step is to convince him this does not have to be the case. Brainwash him if necessary, but get him thinking positively about his backhand.

2. Instructors and students alike are responsible for keeping the forehand and backhand equal in proficiency. But what usually happens is the forehand is the first stroke to be taught and it begins to move ahead of the backhand in reliability. During play the student realizes this, and because he wants to win, he begins to favor the forehand. The more he does this the better it becomes and the backhand falls further and further behind. You and your student should agree to keep the backhand up to or slightly ahead of his forehand in proficiency. If it starts to lag, put more emphasis on it during each lesson, and in turn he must use it more during play.

3. Because of the difference in shoulder position on the backhand versus the forehand, the ball is contacted considerably farther toward the net. This means there is always a split-second less time on the backhand side. Early preparation easily overcomes this, but this must be built into the stroke at the very beginning.

4. On the backhand the arm and wrist have great strength when the ball is contacted well in front of the body, but very little strength when hit late. This is in contrast to the forehand where the arm and wrist maintain their strength

even when the ball is hit late. Make it clear this lack of strength on a late hit, plus the split-second less time to get prepared, means there can be absolutely no compromise on the backhand. He must learn to always be prepared early so he can hit the backhand well in front of him.

Where the Backhand Differs

During previous ground-stroke patterns, you have been working on the twenty basic corrections common to both the forehand and backhand. Now it's time to begin refining the backhand.

There are only five points where the backhand is different from the forehand. As you work these into your instruction, you will find your student will have no problem picking them up. In fact if he has been accomplishing the twenty basic points common to both strokes, the odds are he is already performing these differences quite naturally.

1. The Continental grip should be used on the backhand.
2. The left hand should support and guide the racket through the backswing longer, up to the point the racket starts its descent and forward motion.
3. The wrist is firm and remains unchanged during the entire stroke from ready position through the follow-through.
4. The racket is brought back in a flatter backswing than the forehand. This in turn reduces the size of the arc as the racket moves to hitting level.
5. In the full pivot position the front or right shoulder is far enough around so the point of the shoulder is aiming more toward the left side lines than toward the net. Being the hinge point, the shoulder should remain almost stationary through the hit.

Your student's mental grasp and comprehension of these stroke differences is important. The better he understands the structure of the backhand, the quicker he will learn it, and the easier it will be for him to correct stroke problems that will occasionally crop up in the future. Don't underestimate the importance of why something is done, and don't under-estimate your student's ability to understand and benefit from knowing why.

SPECIAL PROBLEMS TO LOOK FOR—BACKHAND

Arm and Elbow

In bringing the racket back your student will probably have a tendency to keep his upper arm out and away from his body in a horizontal position and then bend his elbow to bring the forearm and racket back. As he starts his forward swing from this position, the elbow will lead the forearm and racket re-sulting in a slapping motion, loss of power and accuracy. To correct this, get your student to bring his upper arm and forearm in close to his body as it comes back with the racket during the pivot. The elbow is only slightly bent. If he has trouble adjusting, ask him to touch his left hip with the inside of his right wrist in the full wind-up position. This will help by giving him a reference point, and although an over-correction, it is very effective. The wrist should remain firm throughout the entire stroke.

Shoulder

The shoulder should be kept down during the backswing and should stay down through the hit. It is the hinge point and to produce full power, needs to be pointing down at the ball. In the full wind-up position he should have his chin tucked in close to, and should be looking over the point of his shoulder.

Hip and Shoulder

The body should move out of the way on the final stage of the stroke thus allowing a free uninterrupted swing. But many players, particularly on the backhand, allow the shoulder and hip to break away much too soon. Because this leads to very serious problems, it is better to teach your student to hold both hip and shoulder a little too long. This is easily adjusted at a later date by getting him to emphasize his follow-through.

Hitting Off the Back Foot

Even if your student is well prepared in advance of the hit, it is possible he can get into the habit of leaving his weight on the back foot as he swings. This causes the shoulder to break upward and the stroke to travel in a golf-type swing. Catch this early and get him moving off the back foot toward the ball, accomplishing full weight transfer to the front foot at the instant of racket contact with the ball. It will also help to get him to emphasize a long forward sweeping follow-through.

Buying Time

Because there can be no compromise in hitting a backhand well in front of the body, a beginner soon learns by backing away from the ball instead of stepping into it, he can buy a couple of split seconds in order to get his racket through. Corrective action must be twofold. First, he must accomplish all the actions of preparation much sooner so when he is in the full backswing position, he is actually waiting for the ball. Second, he must step toward the net with the hitting foot and transfer weight to that foot as the racket hits the ball.

Summary

As your sudent's backhand progresses it should be developing a look of compactness. A wound-spring feeling with stored power ready to use well in advance of the actual hit. From this position he should be unleashing a smoothly accelerating swing and long forward sweeping follow-through ending up pointing toward the top of his opponent's back-stop.

STROKE REFINEMENTS—FOREHAND

Where the Forehand Differs

1. The Eastern grip should be used on the forehand.
2. During the pivot the left hand supports and guides the racket into the backswing until the front or left shoulder reaches its fullest pivot position. As the racket continues on

its way to the full backswing position, the left hand lets go of the racket and extends forward toward the net for balance. The point of the left shoulder is aiming at the net.

3. As the racket moves down to hitting level and starts forward, the shoulders start to rotate. The front shoulder begins to move left and rearward as the right shoulder moves down slightly as it comes forward. At the moment of impact the shoulders will be parallel to the net. Depending on how open the stance, the hips can be either parallel with the net and shoulders, or perpendicular to the net and shoulders and therefore almost parallel to the side line.

4. From the ready position or during the backswing, the wrist is laid back slightly and is firm. It remains this way through the forward swing until the moment of impact. As the racket contacts the ball the wrist moves sharply forward and locks into position so the racket, wrist, and arm form a straight line as the racket sweeps forward in the follow-through. Beginners should not use any wrist and intermediate players should limit this wrist action to the last split second of ball and racket contact, letting the wrist, arm, and racket achieve a straight line in the late stages of the follow-through. If your student is having control problems with his forehand, he is probably using too much wrist. This can be corrected by getting him to make his wrist even firmer through the entire stroke.

5. On the follow-through the shoulders pivot freely allowing the racket to continue its forward and upward sweep.

SPECIAL PROBLEMS TO LOOK FOR—FOREHAND

Grip

Using the wrong grip on the forehand is a problem that can destroy the forehand stroke as the student compensates the resulting improper positioning of the racket face by rotating the wrist and arm during the swing. This is not always obvious, for he may be switching to an incorrect grip during his backswing. Corrective action is simply checking frequently to make sure he has the Eastern forehand grip. The best times to do this are at the full backswing position, and immediately following the hit before your student has had a chance to come back to the ready position.

Racket Face

An easy bad habit to get into on the forehand is closing the racket face. During the backswing the racket face moves from perpendicular to looking down at the playing surface. This can be seen at the full backswing position and should be corrected by asking your student to keep the face of the racket perpendicular throughout the entire stroke. If the problem persists, overcorrect by getting him to open the racket face skyward slightly.

Wrist Not Firm

A weak, wobbly wrist results in an ineffective shot that often doesn't make it over the net. If not corrected, this habit eventually leads to slapping at the ball in an attempt to get some power into the shot. Remind your student of the importance of the wrist being very firm and locked into place at the hit as full weight transference occurs from the back foot to the front foot.

Too Much Wrist

Too much wrist results in a high degree of inaccuracy mixed with an occasional shot going like a bullet in what, to the inexperienced eye, looks like a perfect stroke. Here again emphasis should be placed on firming up the wrist. If the habit continues, the laying back of the wrist during the backswing should be minimized or temporarily eliminated.

Shoulders and Hips

Opening up too soon with the shoulders and hips results in the racket trailing the shoulder pivot. The student will slice or foul off shots to his right and may attempt to overcome this by slapping his wrist forward. There is a simple corrective action. During the backswing he should be letting go of the racket with his left hand and extending his arm forward. When he does this, get him to point at the oncoming ball with his left hand. This helps to keep the shoulders perpendicular to the net until the racket leads them around during the forward swing.

Arm and Elbow

A common problem with beginners and intermediates is a very short follow-through caused by bending the elbow and pulling the racket upward at the hit point instead of sweeping forward through the hit. This habit has a way of getting worse, and soon the racket will be ending up over the left shoulder. Explain to your student the importance of a long sweeping follow-through. Remind him that his arm should fully extend during the follow-through even though the elbow does not lock. Get him to finish the stroke with his racket pointing at the top of his opponent's back-stop.

Summary

As your student's forehand improves it should have the feeling of smooth power with a long sweeping follow-through. His footwork should allow him to step forward into the ball thus allowing him to hit cross-courts and down the line shots with equal power and accuracy.

PATTERNS—STROKE REFINEMENT, BACKHAND AND FOREHAND

When you work on backhand and forehand stroke refinements you will want to concentrate first on one stroke and then the other, but don't hit all the shots of the pattern series to that stroke. In other words, hit at least one of the pattern shots to the stroke not being worked on.

As your student begins to conquer the ground-stroke refinements, he should be fast approaching the point of becoming a good player. Therefore you will need to increase the difficulty of the patterns in order to keep him interested and his game improving at a steady pace. This can be done by increasing the speed of your shots, decreasing the time element between each shot, and by hitting the shots farther away from each other. But one of the most effective ways of increasing pattern difficulty is to get your student to hit more and more of his pattern returns cross-court. This results in by far the most difficult pattern series and is the making of a winning player, for the ability to hit cross-courts from almost any position keeps an opponent from moving over to cover the easier down-the-line return. To hit cross-court returns, your student must be stroking the ball very well indeed. Most important, he will have had to "turn the corner" prior to intercepting the ball so that his weight can move forward through the hit toward the center of the net, rather than down the side line toward the net post.

CHAPTER SIX

MODIFIED GROUND STROKES

Once your student has grooved his basic ground strokes to the point they do not break down under the pressure of fairly tough patterns, you should start to work on the supplementary shots. The word supplementary, which is most often used in describing these shots, can be misleading, for these modified basic strokes are a very important part of a winning player's game. They are the lob, drop shot, half-volley, and serve return. They are as much a part of the basic game as the overhead or serve. You should make sure your student understands this so he will be willing to spend the time necessary to master these modified ground strokes.

The Serve Return

To fully appreciate the extreme importance of the serve return, it helps to look first at the serve. The objective of the serve is to win the point with an outright ace, or to at least set the stage for the eventual winning of the point by placing the receiver in a defensive position from which he never recovers. The serve return must neutralize the effect of the serve or the odds of winning the point remain heavily in favor of the server. Therefore, in terms of importance, the serve return ranks right at the top of the list along with the serve. It also ranks with the serve in terms of degree of difficulty.

The serve-return stroke is greatly affected by the speed,

spin, and placement of the serve as well as by the playing surface, the server's intended court position on his next shot, the server's over-all game, and finally by the serve returner's ability to handle his opponent's serve that day. Depending on these variables, the degree of modification of the basic ground stroke of a serve return may be large or small.

A difference between the serve return and other ground strokes is the ball is not in play until the serve is hit; therefore the receiver has plenty of time to get set. His ready-position grip and stance should be the same as covered in detail in the chapter on ground strokes with two minor differences. First, the knees should be bent more so he will already be down in case the ball comes off low and fast (*Figure 47*). Second, court position should be determined by a line drawn from the server to the receiver, with this line bisecting the angle created by the sharpest angled forehand and sharpest angled backhand serves that can be hit. The receiver's position along this bisecting line may be behind the base line, just in front of it, or several feet in front of it, depending on the variables previously mentioned.

Standing a foot or two inside the base line and catching the serve early gives the receiver a big edge if he can pull it off. It greatly reduces the effective angle of a well-placed serve, and in addition gets the serve return headed back to the receiver's court much sooner. It also allows the receiver to chip the ball, placing the return low at the feet of a net rusher. But the receiver cannot always get away with this preferred serve-return position. If the court surface is particularly fast, if the server is hitting with good speed and placement, or if the receiver's reflexes are not quite up to par, then there will be too many serve-return errors. The serve returner will have to compromise, giving ground and buying time by moving back. By standing behind the base line, he gains valuable split seconds to prepare for the hit, but a well-angled serve pulls him farther out of court and, because he is hitting from a deeper court position, his opponent gains time to get into a better position for his next shot.

Figure 47. The pace of the serve return is determined by how much body weight the receiver can get in behind the hit. The split second the serve is hit he must move and move fast.

HITTING THE SERVE RETURN

As the server tosses the ball, the receiver's concentration should be at its height. He should be ready to move very quickly, in fact considerably quicker than on any other ground stroke. As the server's racket hits the ball, the receiver should move the instant he senses where the serve is headed. His backswing should be started before the ball crosses the net and must be completed before the ball hits in the service court. The farther your student stands in, the less his serve-return stroke will resemble a full ground stroke. The farther he stands in, the less time to execute perfect footwork, and so it is very important that he always pivot his shoulders. His backswing must be very short, similar to the half-volley. He should crowd the ball and get his weight in behind the return. His forward swing will be more of a block, but he must follow through, although not to the extent that he does on a full ground stroke. His wrist will be very firm throughout the entire stroke. It is critical that he watch the ball from the moment of the toss through the hit point of the serve return. The speed or pace of his return comes directly from the amount of body weight he is able to get into the shot.

In the beginning your student will be standing back to return serve, and his stroke will be much closer to a full ground stroke. He still must move very fast, always pivot his shoulders, and in most cases be executing excellent footwork.

SERVE-RETURN PATTERNS

It is difficult to effectively instruct your student on the serve return if you are hitting the serves. It will be well worth enlisting the help of another player who can get valuable serving practice while your student is learning the return. In the beginning ask your server to hit the ball without much speed and have him concentrate on consistency and getting his serve in deep.

Ask your student to take his ready position just behind the

base line. Make sure he is facing the server. This means he will not be standing exactly parallel to the base line. In other words he should face the "problem," which is the server. Many players do not do this, and as a result increase the degree of difficulty of their serve return. You should take up a position on your student's side of the net, moving around occasionally to get a different view.

After several minutes of returning serve from the forehand service court, have your student move over to the backhand court. This not only gives him a chance to learn the serve return from both service courts, but it also gives the server practice in both service courts.

As your student develops his serve return, and he should be working on consistency for quite some time, he can move forward to a ready position just inside the base line. Later you will want to move him in farther to a foot inside the base line. He will need to modify his stroke each time he moves in. As he becomes more and more proficient on the serve return, you will probably have to move up to a better server. Before long you will be enlisting the help of a player or players that have all the serves including an American twist, flat serve, slice, and spin.

You can eventually work in teaching patterns where your student comes into net behind each serve return. When he does you hit him patterns from the base line as your server moves out of the way after hitting the serve. The purpose of this pattern series is to condition your student to taking the net without destroying the consistency of his serve return.

Your next step is to work hard on your student's serve return under playing conditions. Set up practice matches and with agreement from his opponent, take up a position by the net post. When your student is returning serve, watch how he performs the basics. After a point is over, discuss those areas he is not executing properly with particular emphasis on his moving fast, staying down on the ball through the hit, and getting his weight moving in behind the ball toward the net.

SUMMARY

Once your student is accomplishing the basics without having to think about them, he is ready to work on what he should do with his serve return other than just getting it back. The following observations should be discussed with him in detail.

1. His serve return should be reliable, but he should always try to take the offensive any time he can. He should be ready to pounce on a weak serve and blast it, occasionally hitting a drop shot if the server hangs back at the base line.

2. Your student should study his opponent's serve and learn to anticipate the type and direction of the serve he is in the act of hitting. If it is a hard flat serve, your student should be prepared to block it. If it is an American twist, he should move in, catch it early, and chip it.

3. He should learn to anticipate his opponent's "favorite" serve that he uses when he knows he must have the point to avoid a service break.

4. If his opponent is consistently rushing the net, he should move in on the serve, keeping his return low and usually hitting down the side line, but occasionally hitting a lob.

5. He should observe his opponent's handling of his serve returns. He should experiment and find out if a particular type of serve return gives the server trouble. If the server rushes net but only has an adequate overhead, he should lob. If his opponent has trouble changing direction, he should hit his serve returns deep in the corners. If his opponent has trouble handling different spins, he should vary his returns by mixing up backspin and drive returns. If his opponent does not like to come to net, soft well-angled returns can force him to do so.

6. Above all, he should make the server work hard and fight for every point. If your student learns this early and makes it an integral part of his serve return, he will find his opponent's serve will become less and less effective during a match. This allows him to hit an increasingly effective serve

return which puts tremendous additional pressure on his opponent.

The Lob

The lob is most often used as a defensive shot to dislodge an opponent from the net, or to buy time in order to recover from a bad court position. It is also used to safely keep the ball in play when an opponent's shot has been hit excessively hard, or to break up the rhythm of a hard-charging net player. The defensive lob utilizes backspin for control and is a relatively easy shot to hit.

Offensively the lob can be used when an opponent has worked his way into net and has hit a shot that is a little short. He is expecting a solidly hit drive and suddenly the ball is on its way over his head hitting deep in his court near the base line. The key element is surprise. Although the topspin lob is particularly effective in this situation and will result in an outright winner, it is a difficult shot to hit consistently, and therefore is not considered a high percentage shot even by top players. The backspin lob, however, can be used offensively as well as defensively. Like the topspin lob, the key element is surprise, and although it may not result in a clean winner, it puts the opponent in deep trouble from which he seldom recovers.

HITTING THE LOB

The basic forehand or backhand is modified only slightly to hit a backspin lob. The backswing, unless hit under excessive pressure, is the same as when hitting a drive. The racket face, however, is open. At the hit point the racket passes under the ball imparting backspin, which gives control to the shot. The face of the racket remains open during the follow-through which should be forward, upward, and shorter than the usual ground-stroke follow-through.

The topspin lob does not utilize the natural spin on the ball coming off the playing surface as does the backspin lob. In fact it must be hit with sufficient topspin to overcome the playing surface spin and with enough left over to control the ball so that it drops into the court and bounds away toward the opponent's backstop. The spin factor is what makes the topspin lob difficult. For this reason it should not be taught to a student until he is well into the intermediate stage and has developed a consistent and accurate backspin lob. To hit a topspin lob, the racket must start its forward swing from a point below the impact height of the ball. The racket face is slightly closed. The racket continues on a sharp, upward climb ending in a follow-through that is considerably higher than the normal ground stroke. Because of the sharp pull up that is needed to impart the right amount of spin, the topspin lob is exclusively a forehand shot.

LOB PATTERNS

In the beginning you will want to stick with easy alternating patterns until your student is hitting lobs with good consistency off of both sides. Don't ignore the basics just because he is hitting a lob. Watch his preparation and most particularly the footwork. Make sure he does not begin to step backward as he executes the shot. Once he is hitting the lob well off easy patterns, begin to move him around. You can start mixing in short pattern shots with deeper ones. The final step is to have him vary his returns hitting both drives and lobs. Mix in some deep pattern shots with some pace on the ball and see how he handles the lob under pressure.

When your student has progressed to the point you want him to learn the topspin lob, you can continue to use alternating patterns, but he should only hit a topspin lob on his forehand side and the pattern shot should be one that he is not forced on and therefore could comfortably hit as a drive if he wished.

The Drop Shot

The drop shot is an aggressive attack shot that will result in an outright winner. Unlike any other shot it remains on the mind of the opponent like salt in the wound. It can irritate him, break up his rhythm and concentration. Like the offensive lob, the key is surprise.

HITTING THE DROP SHOT

The drop shot is hit with backspin very much like the backspin lob except that it is a much softer shot and the follow-through is not carried upward. It is important to maintain a good follow-through, gentle though it may be. The drop shot should be made with a comfortable margin of safety over the net and should never land in the opponent's court much farther than 7 feet from the net. It must not be hit from any deeper than inside the service line, and only then when the opponent is behind his base line. The more your student's drop shot stroke looks like his regular ground stroke, the more effective it will be.

DROP SHOT PATTERNS

Move your student into mid-court and hit him easy alternating patterns. In the beginning you can hit these from the service line area, but eventually you will want to move back to the base line. Once he has the feel of the drop shot it is important for him to mix his pattern returns so no matter what pattern sequence you use, he is hitting drives and drop shots alternately on both the backhand and forehand. Only in this way can he build a drop shot that looks like a drive remaining disguised until it is too late for the opponent to recover.

The Half-volley

Whether it is hit on the way to net or from a base line position, the half-volley is a combination of partly a ground stroke, partly a volley and always a shot the player should have preferred to hit as one or the other. In other words, the half-volley is never hit through choice, but rather through being caught in a less than desirable situation. The objective of the half-volley is to get out of that situation by floating the ball accurately and deep enough so the opponent is not fed a setup.

HITTING THE HALF-VOLLEY

The basic ground stroke is greatly modified on the mid-court half-volley. Preparation time is very short. The ball must be lifted over the net because it is hit close to the playing surface from a court position somewhere near the service line. To further increase the degree of difficulty, the ball has not had a chance to lose speed or spin and is usually a heavy shot to handle.

Either of two grips can be used on the forehand half-volley, the Continental or the Eastern forehand grip. The Continental grip is the same as used on the volley and the serve and therefore has two advantages. First, most half-volleys occur as a player follows his serve to net and when trapped into a forehand half-volley, he does not have to change grips. Second, after hitting either a forehand or backhand half-volley with the Continental grip, he is ready for a full volley without changing grips. Elimination of these two grip changes may seem minor, but it reduces errors by saving valuable split seconds when preparation time is particularly critical.

When a player moving into net is trapped into hitting a half-volley, his footwork is greatly determined by his relative position to the ball. If it is wrong, there just is not enough time to take an additional step. In fact, if there is enough time to take an extra step, he should move in and hit a full volley.

Regardless of awkward footwork and lack of time, the shoulder pivot must always be accomplished. However, the shoulders do not turn as far as on the ground strokes and the racket should not be brought back past the player's side. In other words, the footwork, pivot, and backswing are condensed to the bare minimums.

On the forehand half-volley the wrist is laid back during the short backswing and is kept firmly in that position through the entire stroke including the follow-through. On the backhand side the wrist position is the same as on the backhand and also remains firm through the entire stroke.

As stroke preparation is completed, the player should be way down to the level of the ball and should stay down through the hit. This is particularly important on the half-volley as it is the only way the racket can be kept parallel with the playing surface, which in turn is key to hitting the half-volley consistently. It is not uncommon to see a player's knee only a few inches from the playing surface.

Whenever possible the ball should be contacted well in front and body weight should move into the shot as the racket travels forward in a smooth positive short stroke. It is very important to impress upon your student the half-volley is never hit hard and its mission is simply to get him out of an undesirable court position which he moves from the instant the shot is completed.

The angle of the racket face varies greatly depending on where the half-volley is being made from and what kind of speed and spin the ball is carrying just prior to racket contact. If it is a hard topspin shot in the service line area, the racket face will have to be closed to keep the half-volley return in court. If it is a soft shot hitting closer to the net the racket face will have to be open. With practice your student will instinctively begin to adjust to the proper racket-face angle.

HALF-VOLLEY PATTERNS

Move your student to a position just behind the service line and begin with easy alternating patterns that hit just in front of him. Keep the shots in close to him so he does not have to go wide toward the side lines. As he gets the feel of the half-volley and is performing the basics consistently you should begin to vary the speed and spin on the ball. You can hit these patterns to your student from the base line, but if you have difficulty in placing them, move into your service line area.

The next step in learning the half-volley is to move your student back to the base line and start each pattern from this new position. The first ball of the pattern will be an easy shot he will play as a full ground stroke, but he will follow it to net. As he starts in, hit your next shot a little sooner than usual thus trapping him into hitting a half-volley. After he hits the half-volley he should move right into net taking the last two shots of the pattern as full volleys. He then returns to the base line and the process is repeated. This series of patterns is particularly effective as your student learns to hit the half-volley in exactly the same circumstances as actual play. If he is having trouble with the half-volley or the full volleys that follow, repeat the same pattern over again until he gets it nailed down.

When your student is handling these patterns well, it is time to have him take a bucket of balls and head for his normal serving position. You take a bucket of balls and take up a position on your base line as if you were going to return serve. Have him serve and come into net. You hit the first shot of the pattern series soon enough to force him into hitting a half-volley. He should immediately follow it into net hitting the last two shots of the pattern series from that position. Vary the pace of your shots and even throw in an occasional lob. You will probably uncover a particular half-volley pattern that gives him trouble. Pattern Play Teaching will bring him through this quickly if you hit the exact same pattern over and over. Once he has mastered the "trouble" pattern, move on to new combinations.

THE BASE LINE HALF-VOLLEY

When your student's game has progressed to the advanced intermediate stage, you can work with him on mastering the base line half-volley. Although seldom used, it is a shot top players can hit any time they need to. The stroke is effective when a player is caught out of position by a particularly deep shot. Instead of backing up and hitting it on a normal bounce from deep behind the base line, the player steps in catching the ball on the rise close to the playing surface. In this way he maintains a good court position and greatly shortens the time his opponent has to get ready for his return.

The base line half-volley is hit with the same stroke as the mid-court half-volley with two minor differences. First, instead of the volley grip the standard ground-stroke grips are used, and second, the follow-through should be slightly longer to assure the necessary depth. As with the mid-court half-volley, the follow-through should remain parallel with the court surface and the player should stay way down on the ball through the hit.

When hitting patterns, have your student crowd the base line and place your pattern shots just inside of it, thus forcing him to play the ball on the rise. You can hit these to him from net. As with the mid-court half-volley, you should vary speed, spin, and trajectory once your student is handling easy alternating patterns.

CHAPTER SEVEN

CHOOSING A RACKET

As observers see the improvement in your student's game, they will ask you many questions. One you will hear repeatedly is "What kind of racket should I buy?"

The reason is the choice has become difficult due to the introduction of many new products ranging from twisted nylon strings that play almost as well as gut, to a wide variety of rackets of wood, various metals and metal fiberglass laminates. To further complicate the problem, at most sport shops, the knowledge of the salesman is limited to selling rackets not playing with them. He will try to sell the most expensive racket he can, because that is his job. Tennis shops usually have better informed sales people who must know their products in order to do well as a specialty store. A brief conversation will quickly determine just how much they do know. In any case it's up to the buyer to know what he wants and how much he should spend.

It can be fun taking practice swings in the store with various shiny new models, each promising great winning shots, but the moment of truth comes after the racket has been chosen, strung, and paid for. Even the more experienced players are often disappointed with their choice after hitting with it. The answer is not how much the buyer has played, but rather, has he learned what to look for when buying a racket? As the price of a good racket is getting up there, it's worth learning.

Metal Versus Wood

The basic difference between a wood racket and metal rests on the simple fact you give something to get something. At the wood end of the spectrum is accuracy and "feel". At the metal end, is speed. In between these extremes are some metal rackets that play more like wood rackets and other metal rackets that are whippy and therefore fall at the speed end of the spectrum. A second difference is wood will age thus losing some of its liveliness, while a metal racket does not age at all.

The job of picking the right racket is a decision which should be based on the player's age, proficiency, type of surface usually played, and so on. The choice should not be based on the fact a particular championship player does or does not play with wood, laminate, or all metal racket. As a matter of fact, championship players have their favorites and it is interesting to note that these span the entire spectrum from all metal to all wood. Therefore, the choice of a racket should be based on a personal evaluation of the individual who will be using it. To help simplify this evaluation, here are some general guidelines that can be applied.

STARTING AT THIRTY YEARS OLD

If a thirty-year-older is starting to learn the game, nine out of ten times the decision should be metal.

1. Physically the metal racket is easier to move.
2. It greatly reduces the shock of the ball hitting the racket even on mis-hits, and helps reduce shoulder problems and tennis elbow.
3. Part of the fun of playing tennis is zinging one in for a winner and the more whippy metal racket imparts extra speed even if a shot is not perfectly timed.
4. For players who are in this group the drawbacks to a metal

racket are greatly outnumbered by the advantages, particularly for women who benefit the most from racket maneuverability and the additional speed imparted to the ball.

STARTING AS A YOUNGSTER

If a youngster, girl or boy, is starting the game, a good-quality wood racket right off the shelf and already strung is an excellent first purchase. Name-brand rackets are sold this way, are adequate to start learning with, and are considerably less expensive. Even though off the shelf, it is still a good idea to choose the right handle size and proper weight. Selections in the sports departments of major chain stores are usually large enough to do this.

If the beginner starts to show real interest and determination, his game will improve, and when this progress becomes obvious it is time to move up to a more expensive racket.

There are several good reasons for staying with a wood racket.

1. His game will change as he grows up, and just like clothes he'll outgrow his racket in grip and weight. Wooden rackets, even good ones, are less expensive than metal.
2. While imparting more speed, metal rackets also produce more errors, and yet one of the biggest battles for the youngster is becoming consistent. The wood racket helps.
3. If a youngster has a particularly strong desire to become good, he may also have a temper problem. Again, the wooden racket is considerably cheaper to replace. The same is true for rackets that become lost.
4. Developing sound strokes in a youngster means weeding out stroke problems before they become firm habits. Whippy metal rackets hide errors in stroke production and make the weeding out process considerably more difficult.

SOMEWHERE IN BETWEEN

If a player falls in between the thirty-year-old group and

the youngster group, the choice of a racket should be based on the following considerations.

1. If he has been playing with a wood racket for several years and is more or less content with his game, the chances are he will improve his game by going to a metal laminate or all metal racket. If he does, he must be willing to stay with this new racket through a learning period. He will find it initially creates errors, but these will diminish and the "winners" will increase as he becomes accustomed to it.

2. Whether a player is just starting out or has been playing for years, if he wants to work hard and improve his game, it is important for him to know if a ball was or was not well hit. A whippy racket makes this more difficult. Even if he does sense he is doing something wrong it can disguise what the real problem actually is, making it just that much tougher to correct. Therefore a wood racket or metal that plays close to a wood racket is a logical choice.

3. And finally, if a player is just starting out or plays occasionally and simply wants to enjoy the game on a casual basis, a metal or a laminate is the probable choice.

Weight

After choosing the type of racket best suited to his game, the buyer must next decide on the weight of the racket.

Judging what weight is best is once again a personal evaluation. Like knowing what size suit or dress to buy, racket weight depends on the size and strength of the individual. In addition, the more often an individual plays, the better physical condition he will be in, and this means a heavier racket can be used. One woman world champion used rackets from the light category up to a fairly hefty medium-weight racket depending on how much she was playing.

To someone just starting, racket weight will have little effect on his ability to hit the ball. As his proficiency increases he will begin to become aware of the difference between one racket and another and will eventually know how these differences affect his game. In deciding on the best weight there are some general guidelines that can be helpful.

Rackets are labeled by manufacturers as "light," "medium," and "heavy," but unfortunately they do not have set weights for these categories. What is labeled as heavy by one manufacturer can be labeled as medium weight by another. In addition these are unstrung weights. By arbitrarily assigning specific *strung* racket weights to these three categories they become more useful as buying guides:

Light	up to 12¼ ounces
Medium	12½ to 13½ ounces
Heavy	13¾ to 14½ ounces

YOUNGSTERS

Rackets for youngsters will fall in the light category with some overlapping into the medium category by ¼ ounce if the youngster is big for his age.

GIRLS

Girls will find the best weight rackets at the lower end of the medium category, up to 13 ounces.

BOYS AND WOMEN

Rackets for boys and women will also fall in the medium-weight category but will be at the heavier end of the scale, up to 13½ ounces, and for a particularly strong individual, up to 13¾ ounces.

MEN

Because of their wide range of strength and size, men will find rackets in the medium category all the way through the heavy category. Many of the top players who are small in stature play with fairly light medium-weight rackets. As a final guideline it should be added that a racket of 14½ ounces is heavy even for a man of considerable size and strength.

Although the well-equipped tennis shop usually has a sensitive scale to weigh rackets, some do not. A good-quality home postal scale should be taken along just in case. The scale may bring a few curious glances, but it is the answer to getting the correct weight of a racket.

If the racket is off the shelf and already strung it can be weighed as is. If it is unstrung, a special weight device consisting of a small weight attached to a wide rubber band should be slipped over the head of the racket. This temporarily substitutes the additional ¾ ounce the strings will add to the frame once the racket is strung. In addition to helping determine the exact weight of a racket, this same device must be used when determining balance. It is very unlikely a tennis shop does not have this weight device, but if not, then a rubber band with a ¾ ounce weight of some kind attached to it makes a suitable substitute.

Balance

After deciding on racket type and weight, the next decision is balance. Balance is especially important as it is a more sensitive and critical factor than minor weight variances. In other words, two rackets with exactly the same weights but different balance points will play very differently. In contrast two rackets with distinct weight differences but identical balance points will play very much the same.

By far the large majority of good tennis players use evenly balanced rackets. The next most popular balance is light in the head. A heavy-headed racket is least desirable as it is difficult to maneuver for its weight and also tends to carry the head of the racket too fast through the hit and too far after the hit.

Determining the balance point of a racket is simple. First slip the ¾ ounce weight device over the head of the racket, making sure it is positioned in the center of the open space of the racket. If this is not properly done, it will give an incorrect balance point. Next, the racket should be balanced on some object that has a fairly sharp or rounded edge. A pen Scotch taped to the bottom of an inverted ash tray works well. After the racket has been balanced, a grease pencil or Scotch tape can be used to mark the balance point. If a pen or pencil is used, it can end up marring the racket. The final step in determining balance is to measure the distance of the balance point from the exact middle of the racket. Most rackets are 27 inches long and, therefore, an evenly balanced racket will have a balance point 13½ inches from both ends. Although some of the new metal rackets are shorter, the procedure remains the same.

A racket that is light in the head has a balance point closer to the handle. To keep from getting mixed up, the racket should be viewed as having three parts: the head, shaft, and handle. If the head is light, then to even things up, more of the shaft is needed on the head side of the balance point. This moves the balance point away from the mid-point, toward the handle.

Few rackets will have their balance point exactly in the middle, but the balance point should not be more than ¼ inch either side of the mid-point if the buyer is looking for an evenly balanced racket. Obviously, the closer the better. Some tennis shops are equipped to balance a racket exactly as the buyer wishes.

Grip

The final step in choosing a racket is deciding on the right size handle. Too small or large a grip makes it difficult to keep the racket from twisting even on slightly off-center hits.

It is estimated that as high as 80 per cent of all tennis players choose too small a grip, and so if in doubt, the buyer would do better to decide on the next larger size. To make the choice easier there are two guidelines that can be followed.

First, take the racket with the Eastern forehand grip, remembering the fingers should be spread. While holding the racket with this grip, turn your wrist over so you can look at your fingernails. If the grip is the correct size, there will be an open space between the fingertips and the base or fleshy part of the thumb. This space should be wide enough to insert the forefinger of your left hand parallel to the base of the thumb. One side of this forefinger should touch the base of the thumb and the other side should just touch the fingertips, thus comfortably filling the space.

The second guideline is to take a racket, grip it firmly but not in a death grip, and have someone twist the head of the racket. After trying this with several rackets with different handle sizes it will become apparent one size makes it a great deal easier to resist the twisting action.

If during the process of selecting rackets having the correct weight and balance, those remaining do not have the exact grip size, it is possible to build up or shave down the handle. If this is kept to a minimum, weight and balance will be only slightly affected. Most tennis shops are capable of doing this although their selections are usually large enough so this is not necessary.

Stringing a Racket

Once a frame has been selected, all that remains is getting it strung. In this final step, there are two considerations. String tension and the kind of strings to be used.

STRING TENSION

String tension has a dramatic effect on how a racket plays, much more so than the type of strings used. The reason is the tautness of the strings have the same effect on the ball as the tension on a trampoline has on a person bouncing around on its surface. If the tension on a trampoline were increased enough, its surface would become very rigid, virtually eliminating any bounce or spring of the trampoline. The same thing is true of a racket. Therefore, the effect of a whippy steel racket can be reduced by very tight string tension or increased by less tension.

In deciding on string tension, the type of racket being played with is a factor. An equally important factor is the surface being played on. A slow surface, such as clay, slows the ball down during the bounce to the point where a great deal more power is needed during the hit to build the speed of the ball back. String tension from 53 to 58 pounds creates speed through the trampoline effect. Playing with too tight a racket on a slow surface causes the player to overhit in an attempt to get speed on his shots.

On a fast surface, like cement, the ball loses very little speed during its contact with the court and, therefore, string tension of 58 to 63 pounds produces plenty of pace. String tension that is too loose will add some trampoline effect to an already fast ball, thus creating errors.

Some tennis shops do not like to use high string tension when stringing a metal racket as the frame cuts the strings and an unhappy customer is soon back on their doorstep. Still, the buyer is the one using the racket and if a little higher tension than recommended gives him the control he wants, he just ends up getting a patch job or a complete restringing more often.

TYPES OF STRINGS

Nylon and gut are the two materials used in making strings. Gut is preferred by all the top players as it effectively grips the ball during impact, thus producing better control. Many players feel it also has more spring or life than nylon. However, it is more expensive and is easily damaged by moisture. Although it is sold by gauge and weight, it takes a very experienced player to tell the difference between 15 gauge and 15 gauge/light. The simplest yardstick is cost. If the buyer wants the best there is, he says so and pays three or four dollars more to find out if it does make a difference in his game.

Nylon has come a long way since first being introduced and now plays almost as well as gut. Until a player reaches the category of an average club player, he will not be able to tell the difference between the two. Nylon is cheaper, moisture does not bother it, and it will not dry out and snap the way gut will. It comes in a wide variety of colors, including an imitation gut, that takes close scrutiny to tell it isn't. For the player who plays occasionally, is an average club player or below, or wants a spare racket for damp playing conditions, nylon is a durable, economical choice.